The World's Famous Orations

VOL. I
GREECE

432 B.C.—324 B.C.

THE WORLD'S FAMOUS ORATIONS

WILLIAM JENNINGS BRYAN
EDITOR-IN-CHIEF

FRANCIS W. HALSEY
ASSOCIATE EDITOR

IN TEN VOLUMES

Vol. I
GREECE

FUNK and WAGNALLS COMPANY
New York and London

PN
6121
B88
v.1

PREFACE

It is now several years since I began to consider the propriety of making a collection of the famous orations of the world for the benefit of students, and with that purpose in view, wherever an opportunity offered, I have conferred with men who were able and willing to give advice as to the selections. At first my intention was to use only enough orations for a single volume, but I afterward became convinced that the plan suggested to me by the publishers of this collection would be a better one, namely: to select enough of the great orations to fill ten volumes, but so to group them as to permit of division into volumes arranged chronologically as to countries.

In selecting the more important of the great speeches there is little room for the exercise of independent judgment, for mankind has already pronounced verdicts which no editor can ignore. But outside of what may be called the accepted masterpieces, there has been some opportunity for choice, and accordingly for this series orations have been chosen which, considering the man, the subject, and the occasion, were thought likely to be the most useful to those who may desire to study history as portrayed in great forensic efforts.

Despairing of finding the time to make this collection unaided, I gladly availed myself of the opportunity offered by the present publishers to do the work in conjunction with Mr. Francis W. Halsey, whose wide experience has eminently fitted him for such an undertaking. He collected a large amount of material along the lines above indicated and then submitted it to me for my approval or rejection. After examining the collection he had made, covering the history of oratory from the earliest Greeks to the present day, changes in the arrangement were made by me, some of the orations were eliminated and others added. Mr. Halsey, I may add, is entitled to the sole credit for one interesting feature of the collection as it stands —namely, the speeches of North American Indians. As these men were the first American orators, specimens of their eloquence deserve a place in these volumes.

During my recent travels abroad I had many opportunities to consult public men in regard to speeches of the orators of England, Ireland, Scotland and Continental Europe. In the compilation of the work I have been placed under special obligations to the following public men of Europe, to whom I desire here to extend my thanks:

Rt. Hon. Sir Henry Campbell-Bannerman, M. P., the British Prime Minister.

Rt. Hon. Arthur J. Balfour, M. P., formerly Prime Minister.

The Earl of Rosebery, formerly Prime Minister.

Lord Loreburn (Sir Robert Reid), Lord High Chancellor of England.

Rt. Hon. Joseph Chamberlain, M. P., formerly Colonial Secretary.

Lord Robert Cecil, son of the late Marquis of Salisbury.

Rt. Hon. Winston Churchill, M. P., son of the late Lord Randolph Churchill, and now Under-Secretary to the Colonies.

Rt. Hon. Herbert Henry Asquith, M. P., Chancellor of the Exchequer.

Rt. Hon. Herbert J. Gladstone, M. P., son of the late William E. Gladstone, and now Home Secretary.

Rt. Hon. James Bryce, M. P., Chief Secretary to the Lord Lieutenant of Ireland.

John W. Redmond, Esq., M. P.

John Dillon, Esq., M. P.

John A. Bright, Esq., son of the late Rt. Hon. John Bright.

Viscount Peel, grandson of Sir Robert Peel, Bt. and Speaker of the House of Commons, 1884-95.

C. F. Moberly Bell, Esq., Manager of the London *Times*.

M. Georges Clemenceau, French Minister of the Interior.[1]

Baron D'Estournelles de Constant, Minister Plenipotentiary of France, member of the Court of The Hague.

Count Albert Apponyi, Leader of the National Party and formerly President of the Hungarian House of Representatives.

Franz Kossuth, son of the late Louis Kossuth, and now a deputy in the Hungarian House of Representatives.

WILLIAM JENNINGS BRYAN.

Paris, August 13, 1906.

---

[1] Since the above was written, M. Clemenceau (in October, 1906) has become Prime Minister of France.

INTRODUCTION

The age of oratory has not passed; nor will it pass. The press, instead of displacing the orator, has given him a larger audience and enabled him to do a more extended work. As long as there are human rights to be defended; as long as there are great interests to be guarded; as long as the welfare of nations is a matter for discussion, so long will public speaking have its place.

There have been many definitions of eloquence. Daniel Webster has declared that it consists in the man, in the subject, and in the occasion. No one can question the truth of his statement. Without the man, the subject and the occasion are valueless, but it is equally true that, without a great subject and a proper occasion, a man speaks without effect. The speaker, moreover, is eloquent in proportion as he knows what he is talking about and means what he says. In other words, knowledge and earnestness are two of the most important requisites of successful speaking.

While oratorical ability has, at times, manifested itself in several generations of one family, it can not be said that heredity is an element of importance, for nearly all the great orators of the world have appeared with little or nothing in a preceding generation to give promise of prominence. An orator is largely a product of his environment. One who is born into a great conflict, or is surrounded by conditions which compel study and investigation, and who becomes enthused with a great purpose, soon attracts attention as a speaker. He is listened to because he has something to say; because he himself feels he makes others feel. Because he conceives that he has a mission, he touches and moves those whom he addresses. Eloquent speech is not from lip to ear, but rather from heart to heart.

While it is absolutely necessary for the orator to master his subject and to speak with earnestness, his speech can be made more effective by the addition of clearness, brevity and apt illustrations.

Clearness of statement is of very great importance. It is not sufficient to say that there are certain self-evident truths; it is more accurate to say that all truth is self-evident. Because truth is self-evident, the best service that one can render a truth is to state it so clearly that it can be comprehended; for a truth once comprehended needs no argument in its support. In debate, therefore, one's first effort should be to state his own side so clearly and concisely as to make the principles involved easily understood. His second object should be so to divest his opponent's argument of useless verbiage as to make it stand forth clearly; for as truth is self-evident, so error bears upon its face its own condemnation. Error needs only to be exposed to be overthrown.

Brevity of statement also contributes to the force of a speaker. It is possible so to enfold a truth in long-drawn-out sentences as practically to conceal it. The epigram is powerful because it is full of meat and short enough to be remembered. To know when to stop is almost as important as to know where to begin and how to proceed. The ability to condense great thoughts into small words and brief sentences is an attribute of genius. Often one lays down a book with the feeling that the author has "said nothing with elaboration," while in perusing another book one finds a whole sermon in a single sentence, or an unanswerable argument couched in a well-turned phrase.

The interrogatory is frequently employed by the orator, and when wisely used is irresistible. What dynamic power, for instance, there is in that question propounded by Christ, "What shall it profit a man if he gain the whole world and lose his own soul?" Volumes could not have presented so effectively the truth that he sought to impress upon his hearers.

The illustration has no unimportant place in the equipment of the orator. We understand a thing more easily when we know that it is like something which we have already seen. Illustrations may be drawn from two sources—nature and literature—and of the two, those from nature have the greater weight. All learning is valuable; all history is useful. By knowing what has been we can better judge the future; by knowing how men have acted heretofore we can understand how they will act again in similar circumstances. But people know nature better than they know books, and the illustrations drawn from every-day life are the most effective.

If the orator can seize upon something within the sight or hearing of his audience—something that comes to his notice at the moment and as if not thought of before—it will add to the effectiveness of the illustration. For instance, Paul's speech to the Athenians derived a large part of its strength from the fact that he called attention to an altar near by, erected "to the Unknown God," and then proceeded to declare unto them the God whom they ignorantly worshiped.

Classical allusions ornament a speech, their value being greater of course when addressed to those who are familiar with their source. Poetry can often be used to advantage, especially when the sentiment is appropriate and is set forth in graceful language. By far the most useful quotations for an orator, however, are those from Holy Writ. The people are more familiar with the Bible than with any other single book, and lessons drawn from it reinforce a speech. The Proverbs of Solomon abound in sentences which aptly express living truths. Abraham Lincoln used scripture quotations very frequently and very powerfully. Probably no Bible quotation, or, for that matter, no quotation from any book ever has had more influence upon a people than the famous quotation made by Lincoln in his Springfield (Ill.) speech of 1858,— "A house divided against itself can not stand." It is said that he had searched for some time for a phrase which would present in the strongest possible way the proposition he intended to advance—namely, that the nation could not endure half-slave and half-free.

The object of public speaking usually is to

persuade. Some one, in describing the difference
between Cicero and Demosthenes, remarked:
"When Cicero spoke people said: 'How well Cicero speaks!' but when Demosthenes spoke they
said, 'Let us go against Philip.' "—the difference
being that Cicero impressed himself upon the
audience, while Demosthenes impressed his subject upon them. Whether or not this comparison be a fair one, it at least presents an important truth. It is a compliment to a public
speaker that the audience should discuss what he
says rather than his manner of saying it; more
complimentary that they should remember his
arguments, than that they should praise his rhet-
oric. The orator should seek to conceal himself
behind his subject. If he presents himself in
every speech he is sure to become monotonous, if
not offensive. If, however, he focuses attention
upon his subject, he can find an infinite number
of themes and, therefore, give variety to his
speech.

In reading great orations one not only learns
something of the mental methods and style of

the orator, but obtains an epitome of the history
of the times. As each important speech is vir-
tually a product of the entire life of the speaker,
so the speeches delivered at great crises in national history have been products of the conditions that called them forth. Nowhere is so much
information crowded into the same number of
words as in a memorable speech. The greatest
of all the orations that have come down to us
from the past is the one by Demosthenes, known
as "The Oration on the Crown," which is included in the volume on Greece in this series. It
possesses every requisite. It is persuasive; it is
argumentative, and the arguments are so skilfully
arranged as to produce the greatest effect; it is
clear in statement; it is eloquent and contains
passages that can not be surpassed in invective;
and it abounds in definitions and distinctions
which are as valuable to-day as when they were
uttered.

The reader will note the appeal which Demosthenes made to the sense of justice, to which
all arguments should be addressed. He called

attention at the beginning to the well recognized fact that his own risk was greater than that of Æschines; for while the latter could, at most, suffer some disappointment at failure in the prosecution, he (Demosthenes), if he lost would forfeit the regard of his people. And as he appeared in his own defense, he reminded them that people take more pleasure in hearing invective and accusations than in hearing a man praise himself; and yet if he, himself, did not set forth the arguments to be made in his own behalf, he would be without defense.

The definition which Demosthenes gives of the statesman is worth remembering. He says:

"Yet understand me. Of what a statesman may be responsible for I allow the utmost scrutiny; I deprecate it not. What are his functions? *To observe things in the beginning, to foresee and foretell them to others,—this I have done: again, wherever he finds delays, backwardness, ignorance, jealousies, vices inherent and unavoidable in all communities, to contract them into the narrowest compass, and, on the other hand, to promote unanimity and friendship and zeal in the discharge of duty. All this, too, I have performed."*

Statesmanship not only requires a knowledge of the principles that control human beings, but it also requires moral courage. Demosthenes understood the demands upon a statesman and satisfied his audience that he had been equal to these demands.

In the discussion of bribery Demosthenes presented a thought which may well be borne in mind: "But by refusing the price of corruption I have overcome Philip; for as the offerer of a bribe, if it be accepted, has vanquished the taker, so the person who refuses it and is not corrupted, has vanquished the person offering." No one has ever thrown a stronger light on the subject of bribery, or more accurately stated the relation between the man who gives and the man who accepts a bribe.

When I was a young man I bought a ten-volume set of orations in order to obtain one speech, and that speech was valuable to me because it contained one sentence. The speech referred to was the one by Pericles,[1] on those who had died in the Peloponnesian War. The sentence reads: "It was for such a country then that these men, nobly resolving not to have it taken from them, fell fighting; and every one of their survivors may well be willing to suffer in its behalf."

Having described the glories of Greece and the advantages of the government, he pointed out that her people, recognizing the blessings of citizenship, were willing to die rather than surrender those blessings. He thus states, in a few words, the secret of a nation's strength—love of country, justified by the government's care for the welfare of the people.

One of the speeches of Socrates as reported by Plato contains a noble paragraph which rebukes the worldly-minded of to-day. It presents a lofty ideal of life and deserves to be committed to memory:

"O Athenians, I honor and love you; but I shall obey God rather than you; and as long as I breathe and am able I shall not cease study-

---

[1] It will be found in volume one of this series.

ing philosophy and exhorting you and warning any one of you I may happen to meet, saying, as I have been accustomed to do, 'O best of men, seeing you are an Athenian of a city the most powerful and most renowned for wisdom and strength, are you not ashamed of being careful for riches, how you may acquire them in greatest abundance, and for glory and honor, but care not nor take any thought for wisdom and truth, and for your soul, how it may be made most perfect?' "

The speeches of Cicero rank next to those of Demosthenes in their wealth of lessons to the student of oratory. All the vast learning of the great Roman was used to illumine his forensic efforts. The speech against Verres, which will be found in the volume devoted to Roman speeches, is generally regarded as the one which best displays his varied talents.

As my object has been to make this collection as useful as possible, I have included the fragments that have come down to us of the memorable speeches of the Gracchi and the defense of his own humble birth made by Caius Marius to the people of Rome. The following from Tiberius Gracchus gives a glimpse of the conditions that called forth the eloquence of the Gracchi and shows also how largely a man's work is shaped by the times in which he lives:

"The wild beasts of Italy have their caves to retire to, but the brave men who spill their blood in her cause, have nothing left but air and light. Without houses, without settled habitations, they wander from place to place with their wives and children; and their generals do but mock them when, at the head of their armies, they exhort their men to fight for their sepulchers and the gods of their hearths: for among such numbers, perhaps there is not one Roman who has an altar that has belonged to his ancestors, or a sepulcher in which their ashes rest. The private soldiers fight and die, to advance the wealth and luxury of the great; and they are called masters of the world, without having a sod to call their own."

More than one of those who peruse these volumes may have had occasion to make a defense similar to that of Marius, but it is doubtful whether one better than his was ever offered. It includes the following words:

"They despise my humbleness of birth; I contemn their imbecility. My condition is made an objection to me; their misconduct is a reproach to them. The circumstances of birth, indeed, I consider as one and the same to all; but think that he who best exerts himself is the noblest. If the patricians justly despise me, let them also despise their own ancestors, whose nobility, like mine, had its origin in merit. They envy me the honor that I have received; let them also envy me the toils, the abstinence, and the perils by which I obtained that honor."

If space permitted quotations might be made from other speeches here given, for each has its own distinctive merits. In Sheridan's speech at the trial of Warren Hastings, the reader will find some excellent examples of invective. I must quote a single passage from that speech:

"If a stranger had at this time [in 1782] gone into the kingdom of Oude, ignorant of what had happened since the death of Sujah Dowlah, that man who with a savage heart had still great lines of character, and who with all his ferocity in war, had still with a cultivating hand preserved to his country the riches which it derived from benignant skies, and a prolific soil—if this stranger, ignorant of all that had happened in the short interval, and observing the wide and general devastation, and all the horrors of the scene—of plains unclothed and brown—of vegetation burnt up and extinguished—of villages depopulated and in ruin—of temples unroofed and perishing—of reservoirs broken down and dry—he would naturally inquire, What war had thus laid waste the fertile fields of this once beautiful and opulent country? What civil dissensions have happened thus to tear asunder, and separate the happy societies that once possessed those villages? What religious rage had, with unholy violence, demolished those temples, and disturbed fervent, but unobtruding piety in the exercise of its duties? What merciless enemy had thus spread the horrors of fire and sword? What severe visitation of Providence had thus dried up the mountains, and taken from the face of the earth every vestige of green?—or rather, what monsters had crawled over the country, tainting and poisoning what the voracious appetite could not devour? To such questions, what must be the answer? No wars have ravaged these lands and depopulated these villages—no civil discords have been felt—no religious rage—no merciless enemy—no affliction of Providence, which, while it scourged for the moment, cut off the sources of resuscitation—no voracious and poisoning monsters—no; all this has been accomplished by the friendship, generosity and kindness of the English nation. They have embraced us with their protecting arms—and, lo, these are the fruits of their alliance."

There is much that the public speaker can study to advantage in the orations of Burke, O'Connell and Gladstone. The parliamentary struggles of Great Britain and Ireland have naturally resulted in the development of many masters in the art of speech, but the nations of Continental Europe have not been overlooked in the selections here made. It has been the intention to give both sides in every contest fairly. The speech of Æschines against Demosthenes is given, as well as the unrivaled defense offered by the greatest orator of ancient Greece. Cicero's speech against Catiline is accompanied by extracts from the speeches of Catiline. So, too, are given the speeches of Cæsar and Cato for and against the punishment by death of the Catiline conspirators.

The same rule has been followed in English and American politics. Particular care has been taken to present both sides of a great controversy in the speeches of representative men. Burke, Chatham and Mansfield represent the divided English sentiment in the American Revolution; Pitt and Fox, English sentiment as to treating with Napoleon as First Consul; Gladstone and Beaconsfield, their respective parties in England's own affairs; while Mr. Chamberlain speaks for the conservative government recently overthrown; and Sir Henry Campbell-Bannerman outlines the policy of the new Liberal government.

I have thought it wise to include by his permission, as representing the present Prime Minister still further, the speech delivered by Sir

Henry at the opening of the recent London session of the Interparliamentary Union. That speech is not only characterized by lofty ideas, but presents a strong argument in favor of peace and moreover it contains one of the most thrilling sentences uttered by a statesman in office in modern times. Representatives of the Russian Duma were present at this session of the Interparliamentary Union, but the Duma had been dissolved after they left home. In referring to the fact that this dissolution had been accompanied by the promise of a new election, the Prime Minister paraphrased a sentence long used in reference to Kings and Emperors and declared, "The Duma is dead; long live the Duma." The audience which was then assembled in the Royal gallery of the British House of Lords rose as one man, the cheers indicating that the speaker had touched a responsive chord.

It has been impossible to include in three volumes all the American orations which might be deemed worthy of a place, but important periods have been covered, and the main issues presented. Hearing is given to Jefferson, and to his political opponent Hamilton, the two representing opposite schools of political thought. The speeches of Webster and Hayne, on the right of a state to secede, are given, as well as speeches from Webster, Clay and Calhoun on the Compromise of 1850. The slave issue is defined by its ablest representatives. For example, the speech of Charles Sumner which provoked the assault of Preston Brooks and the speech of Brooks in justification of himself have been included. We have been careful to reproduce the speeches made in the first of the series of joint debates in Illinois between Lincoln and Douglas which are the most celebrated political debates in history. The subject of the debate was one which stirred the nation to its very depths, and the participants became only two years later, opposing candidates for the highest office within the gift of the people.

As orators the two men were well matched, altho they were entirely different in style and method; they spoke to immense crowds, and

their speeches were accepted as the best statements of their respective sides. Lincoln had an
advantage, in that he could oppose the principle
of slavery without threatening interference with
it where it already existed under the Constitution; and yet so strong was Douglas's presenta-
tion that he defeated Lincoln in the senatorial
contest then pending, only to be defeated by him
two years later in the contest for the Presidency.
Every student of oratory should secure a complete copy of the debates between these two
giants. The debate selected for this collection
being the first (the one at Ottawa), gives a fair
example of the oratory of each. The first inaugural address of Lincoln and the farewell addresses of Jefferson Davis and Robert Toombs
when they withdrew from the Senate reflect the
attitude of the North and South at that time.

The tariff question is discussed in the speeches
of Speaker Crisp, and ex-Speaker Reed, each a
well-equipped champion of his party, while the
money question finds worthy exponents in Senator John Sherman and Congressman Richard

P. Bland, who for nearly twenty years were the leaders of the opposing forces on this subject.

Among the American orations is one by the great historian, Bancroft, on "The people in Art, Government and Religion." So far as my reading goes, this is the most splendid tribute ever paid to the common people in an oration. It is full of sentences that could be quoted as texts.

Only two living American orators have been included—these being ex-President Cleveland and President Roosevelt, who are in a class by themselves. By his permission, Mr. Cleveland's first inaugural address and his remarks to the students of Princeton University on the assassination of President McKinley are given. President Roosevelt is represented by his inaugural address and by his speech at the Mothers' Congress, the selection of the latter having been made after consultation with him.

WILLIAM JENNINGS BRYAN.

Paris, August 13, 1906.

CONTENTS

Vol. I—Greece (432 B.C.—324 B.C.)

	Page
PREFACE	v
INTRODUCTION	x
ACHILLES—His Reply to the Envoys (Legendary)	3
PERICLES—I In Favor of the Peloponnesian War (432 B.C)	9
II On Those Who Died in the War (430 B.C.)	16
III In Defense of Himself (430 B.C.)	27
CLEON—On the Punishment of the Mytileneans (427 B.C.)	34
ALCIBIADES—I In Support of the Athenian Expedition to Sicily (414 B.C.)	41
II To the Spartans (413 B.C.) .	47
NICIAS—Against the Sicilian Expedition (414 B.C.)	49
HERMOCRATES—On the Union of Sicily Against Invaders (416 B.C.) . . .	55
LYSIAS—Against Eratosthenes (403 B.C.) . .	61

CONTENTS

	Page
SOCRATES—I In His Own Defense (399 B.C.)	65
II On Being Declared Guilty (399 B.C.)	77
III On Being Condemned to Death (399 B.C.)	82
ISOCRATES—On the Union of Greece to Resist Persia (380 B.C.)	89
ISAEUS—In the Suit Against Dicæogenes and Leochares	101
DEMOSTHENES—I The Second Oration Against Philip (344 B.C.)	110
II On the State of the Chersonesus (342 B.C.)	120
III On the Crown (330 B.C.)	143
AESCHINES—Against Ctesiphon; or, On the Crown (330 B.C.)	186
DINARCHUS—Against Demosthenes (324 B.C.)	233

VOL. I

GREECE

432 B.C.—324 B.C.

ACHILLES

HIS REPLY TO THE ENVOYS[1]
(LEGENDARY)

Date of Homer's birth and death unknown, but 800 to 900 B.C. the
period usually accepted. Of the seven cities contending for the
honor of having been his birthplace, Smyrna possesses the best
evidence. Many critics contend that the poems bearing Homer's
name were written by various persons in different ages, but it is
probable that at least the Iliad, or a considerable part of it, was
the product of a single mind.

HEAVEN-SPRUNG son of Laertes, Odysseus of
many wiles, in openness must I now declare
unto you my saying, even as I am minded and
as the fulfilment thereof shall be, that ye may
not sit before me and coax this way and that.
For hateful to me, even as the gates of hell,
is he that hideth one thing in his heart and
uttereth another; but I will speak what me
seemeth best. Not me, I ween, nor the other
Danaans, shall Agamemnon, son of Atreus, persuade, seeing we were to have no thank for bat-
tling with the foeman ever without respite. He
that abideth at home hath equal share with him
that fightest his best, and in like honor are held

---

[1] Addressed more particularly to Odysseus, one of the envoys,
than to Phoinix and Ajax, the others. These envoys had been sent
by Agamemnon to plead with Achilles for his return to action in
the war against Troy. The Lang, Leaf and Myers translation.
Printed by arrangement with Macmillan & Co. of London.

both the coward and the brave; death cometh alike to the untoiling and to him that hath toiled long.

Neither have I any profit for that I endured tribulation of soul, ever staking my life in fight. Even as a hen bringeth her unfledged chickens each morsel as she winneth it, and with herself it goeth hard, even so I was wont to watch out many a sleepless night and pass through many bloody days of battle, warring with folk for their women's sake. Twelve cities of men have I laid waste from shipboard, and from land eleven, I do you to wit, throughout deep-soiled Troy-land; out of all these took I many goodly treasures, and would bring and give them all to Agamemnon, son of Atreus, and he staying behind amid the fleet ships would take them and portion out some few but keep the most. Now, some he gave to be meeds of honor to the princes and the kings, and theirs are left untouched; only from me of all the Achaians took he my darling lady and keepeth her—let him sleep beside her and take his joy.

But why must the Argives make war on the Trojans? Why hath Atreides gathered his host and led them hither? Is it not for lovely-haired Helen's sake? Do then the sons of Atreus alone of mortal men love their wives? Surely, whatsoever man is good and sound of mind and loveth his own and cherisheth her, even as I, too, loved mine with all my heart, tho but the captive of my spear. But now that he hath taken my meed of honor from mine arms and hath deceived me, let him not tempt me that know him full well; he shall not prevail.

Nay, Odysseus, let him take counsel with thee and all the princes to ward from the ships the consuming fire. Verily without mine aid he hath wrought many things, and built a wall and dug a foss about it wide and deep, and set a palisade therein; yet even so can he not stay murderous Hector's might. But so long as I was fighting amid the Achaians, Hector had no mind to array his battle far from the wall, but scarce came unto the Skaian gates and to the oak tree; there once he awaited me alone and scarce escaped my onset. But now, seeing I have no mind to fight with noble Hector, I will to-morrow do sacrifice to Zeus and all the gods, and store well my ships when I have launched them on the salt seas. Then shalt thou see, if thou wilt and hast any care therefor, my ships sailing at break of day over Hellespont, the fishes' home, and my men right eager at the oar; and if the great Shaker of the earth grant me good journey, on the third day should I reach deep-soiled Phthia. There are my great possessions that I left when I came hither to my hurt; and yet more gold and ruddy bronze shall I bring from hence, and fair-girdled women and gray iron, all at least that were mine by lot; only my meed of honor hath he that gave it me taken back in his despitefulness, even Lord Agamemnon, son of Atreus.

5

To him declare ye everything even as I charge you, openly, that all the Achaians likewise may have indignation, if happily he hopeth to beguile yet some other Danaan, for that he is ever clothed in shamelessness. Verily not in my face would he dare to look, tho he have the front of a dog. Neither will I devise counsel with him nor any enterprise, for utterly he hath deceived me and done wickedly; but never again shall he beguile me with fair speech. Let this suffice him. Let him begone in peace; Zeus, the lord of counsel, hath taken away his wits. Hateful to me are his gifts, and I hold him at a straw's worth. Not even if he gave me ten times, yea twenty, all that now is his, and all that may come to him otherwhence, even all the revenue of Orchomenos or Egyptian Thebes where the treasure-houses are stored fullest—Thebes of the hundred gates, whence sally forth two hundred warriors through each with horses and chariots —nay, nor gifts in number as sand or dust; not even so shall Agamemnon persuade my soul till he have paid me back at the bitter despite.

And the daughter of Agamemnon, son of Atreus, will I not wed, not were she rival of golden Aphrodite for fairness and for handiwork matched bright-eyed Athene—not even then will I wed her; let him choose him of the Achaians another that is his peer and is more royal than I. For if the gods indeed preserve me and I come unto my home, then will Peleus himself marry me a wife. Many Achaian maidens are there throughout Hellas and Phthia, daughters of princes that rule their cities; whomsoever of these I wish will I make my dear lady. Very often was my high soul moved to take me there a wedded wife, a helpmeet for me, and have joy of the possessions that the old man Peleus possesseth.

For not of like worth with life hold I even all the wealth that men say was possessed of the well-peopled city of Ilios in days of peace gone by, before the sons of the Achaians came; neither all the treasure that the stone threshold of the archer Phoebus Apollo encompasseth in rocky Pytho. For kine and goodly flocks are to be had for the harrying, and tripods and chestnut horses for the purchasing; but to bring back man's life neither harrying nor earning availeth when once it hath passed the barrier of his lips. For thus my goddess mother telleth me, Thetis, the silverfooted, that twain fates are bearing me to the issue of death. If I abide here and besiege the Trojan's city, then my returning home is taken from me, but my fame shall be imperishable; but if I go home to my dear native land, my high fame is taken from me, but my life shall endure long while, neither shall the issue of death soon reach me.

Moreover, I would counsel you all to set sail homeward, seeing ye shall never reach your goal of steep Ilios; of a surety, far-seeing Zeus holdeth his hand over her and her folk are of good courage. So go your way and tell my answer

7

to the princes of the Achaians, even as is the office of elders, that they may devise in their hearts some other better counsel such as shall save them their ships and the host of the Achaians amid the hollow ships; since this counsel availeth them naught that they have now devised by reason of my fierce wrath. But let Phoenix now abide with us and lay him to rest, that he may follow with me on my ships to our dear native land to-morrow, if he will; for I will not take him perforce.

PERICLES

I

IN FAVOR OF THE PELOPONNESIAN WAR [1]

(432 B.C.)

Born about 500 B.C., died in 429; entered public life about 469 as leader of the Democratic party; principal minister of the Athenian State after 444; commanded in the first Peloponnesian War.

I ALWAYS adhere to the same opinion, Athenians, that we should make no concessions to the Lacedæmonians; altho I know that men are not persuaded to go to war, and act when engaged in it, with the same temper; but that, according to results, they also change their views. Still I see that the same advice, or nearly the same, must be given by me now as before; and I claim from those of you who are being persuaded to war, that you will support the common resolutions, should we ever meet with any reverse; or not, on the other hand, to lay any

[1] Delivered before the Assembly at Athens during a discussion of the Lacedæmonian demands. Reported by Thucydides. Translated by Henry Dale.

As to the authenticity of the speeches here taken from Thucydides (those of Pericles, Cleon, Nicias, and Alcibiades), the statement of Thucydides on the subject must be kept in mind: " I have found it difficult to retain a memory of the precise words that I had heard spoken, and so it was with those who brought me report. I have made the persons say what it seemed to me most opportune

claim to intelligence, if successful. For it frequently happens that the results of measures proceed no less incomprehensibly than the counsels of man; and therefore we are accustomed to regard fortune as the author of all things that turn out contrary to our expectation.

Now the Lacedæmonians were both evidently plotting against us before, and now especially are doing so. For whereas it is expressed in the treaty, that we should give and accept judicial decisions of our differences, and each side [in the mean time] keep what we have; they have neither themselves hitherto asked for such a decision, nor do they accept it when we offer it; but wish our complaints to be settled by war rather than by words; and are now come dictating, and no longer expostulating. For they command us to raise the siege of Potidæa, and to leave Ægina independent, and to rescind the decree respecting the Megareans; while these last envoys that have come charge us also to leave the Greeks independent. But let none of you think we should be going to war for a trifle, if we did not rescind the decree respecting the Megareans, which they principally put forward,

for them to say, in view of the situation; at the same time I have adhered as closely as possible to the general sense of what was actually said." R. C. Jebb, discussing this matter, says: "We may be sure that wherever Thucydides had any authentic clue to the actual tenor of the speech, he preferred to follow that clue rather than to draw on his own invention." Jebb adds, that "to these speeches is due, in no small measure, the imperishable intellectual interest of the history."

[saying,] that if it were rescinded, the war would not take place: nor leave in your minds any room for self-accusation hereafter, as tho you had gone to war for a trivial thing. For this trifle involves the whole confirmation, as well as trial, of your purpose. If you yield to these demands, you will soon also be ordered to do something greater, as having in this instance obeyed through fear: but by resolutely refusing you would prove clearly to them that they must treat with you more on an equal footing.

Henceforth then make up your minds, either to submit before you are hurt, or, if we go to war, as I think is better, on important or trivial grounds alike to make no concession, nor to keep with fear what we have now acquired; for both the greatest and the least demand from equals, imperiously urged on their neighbors previous to a judicial decision, amounts to the same degree of subjugation.

Now with regard to the war, and the means possessed by both parties, that we shall not be the weaker side, be convinced by hearing the particulars. The Peloponnesians are men who cultivate their land themselves; and they have no money either in private or public funds. Then they are inexperienced in long and transmarine wars, as they only wage them with each other for a short time, owing to their poverty. And men of this description can neither man fleets nor often send out land armaments; being at the same time absent from their private busi-

ness, and spending from their own resources;
and, moreover, being also shut out from the sea:
but it is superabundant revenues that support
wars, rather than compulsory contributions. And
men who till the land themselves are more ready
to wage war with their persons than with their
money: feeling confident, with regard to the
former, that they will escape from dangers; but
not being sure, with regard to the latter, that
they will not spend it before they have done;
especially should the war be prolonged beyond
their expectations, as [in this case] it probably
may. For in one *battle* the Peloponnesians and
their allies might cope with all the Greeks together; but they could not carry on a *war* against
resources of a different description to their own;
since they have no one board of council, so as to
execute any measure with vigor; and all having
equal votes, and not being of the same races,
each forwards his own interest; for which reasons nothing generally is brought to completion.

Most of all will they be impeded by scarcity
of money, while, through their slowness in providing it, they continue to delay their operations;
whereas the opportunities of war wait for no
one. Neither, again, is their raising works against
us worth fearing, or their fleet. With regard to
the former, it were difficult even in time of peace
to set up a rival city; much more in a hostile
country, and when we should have raised works
no less against them: and if they build [only] a
fort, they might perhaps hurt some part of our

land by incursions and desertions; it will not, however, be possible for them to prevent our sailing to their country and raising forts, and retaliating with our ships, in which we are so strong. For we have more advantage for land-service from our naval skill, than they have for naval matters from their skill by land.

But to become skilful at sea will not easily be acquired by them. For not even have you, tho practising from the very time of the Median War, brought it to perfection as yet; how then shall men who are agriculturists and not mariners, and, moreover, will not even be permitted to practise, from being always observed by us with many ships, achieve any thing worth speaking of? Against a few ships observing them they might run the risk, encouraging their ignorance by their numbers; but when kept in check by many, they will remain quiet; and through not practising will be the less skilful, and therefore the more afraid. For naval service is a matter of art, like anything else; and does not admit of being practised just when it may happen, as a bywork; but rather does not even allow of anything else being a bywork to it.

Even if they should take some of the funds at Olympia or Delphi, and endeavor, by higher pay, to rob us of our foreign sailors, that would be alarming, if we were not a match for them, by going on board ourselves and our resident aliens; but now this is the case; and, what is best of all, we have native steersmen, and crews at large, more numerous and better than all the rest of Greece. And with the danger before them, none of the foreigners would consent to fly his country, and at the same time with less hope of success to join them in the struggle, for the sake of a few days' higher pay.

The circumstances of the Peloponnesians then seem, to me at least, to be of such or nearly such a character; while ours seem both to be free from the faults I have found in theirs, and to have other great advantages in more than an equal degree. Again, should they come by land against our country, we will sail against theirs; and the loss will be greater for even a part of the Peloponnese to be ravaged, than for the whole of Attica. For *they* will not be able to obtain any land in its stead without fighting for it; while *we* have abundance, both in islands and on the mainland. Moreover, consider it [in this point of view]: if we had been islanders, who would have been more impregnable? And we ought, as it is, with views as near as possible to those of islanders, to give up all thought of our land and houses, and keep watch over the sea and the city; and not, through being enraged on their account, to come to an engagement with the Peloponnesians, who are much more numerous; (for if we defeat them, we shall have to fight again with no fewer of them; and if we meet with a reverse, our allies are lost also; for they will not remain quiet if we are not able to lead our forces against them;) and we should make lamentation, not for the houses and land, but for the lives [that are lost] ; for it is not these things that gain men, but men that gain these things. And if I thought that I should persuade you, I would bid you go out yourselves and ravage them, and show the Peloponnesians that you will not submit to them for these things, at any rate.

I have also many other grounds for hoping that we shall conquer, if you will avoid gaining additional dominion at the time of your being engaged in the war, and bringing on yourselves dangers of your own choosing; for I am more afraid of our own mistakes than of the enemy's plans. But those points shall be explained in another speech at the time of the events. At the present time let us send these men away with this answer: that with regard to the Megareans, we will also allow them to use our ports and market, if the Lacedæmonians also abstain from expelling foreigners, whether ourselves or our allies (for it forbids neither the one nor the other in the treaty) : with regard to the states, that we will leave them independent, if we also held them as independent when we made the treaty; and when *they* too restore to the states a permission to be independent suitably to the interests, not of the Lacedæmonians themselves, but of the several states, as they wish: that we are willing to submit to judicial decision, according to the treaty : and that we will not commence hostilities, but will defend ourselves against those who do. For this is both a right answer and a becoming one for the state to give.

But you should know that go to war we must; and if we accept it willingly rather than not, we shall find the enemy less disposed to press us hard; and, moreover, that it is from the greatest hazards that the greatest honors also are gained, both by state and by individual. Our fathers, at any rate, by withstanding the Medes —tho they did not begin with such resources [as we have], but had even abandoned what they had—and by counsel, more than by fortune, and by daring, more than by strength, beat off the barbarian, and advanced those resources to their present height. And we must not fall short of them; but must repel our enemies in every way, and endeavor to bequeath our power to our posterity no less [than we received it].

II

ON THOSE WHO DIED IN THE WAR[1]
(430 B.C.)

THE greater part of those who ere now have spoken in this place, have been accustomed to praise the man who introduced this oration into the law; considering it a right thing that it

---

[1] Delivered "in the fairest suburb" of Athens over the bodies of those who had fallen in the first Peloponnesian War. Reported by Thucydides. Translated by Henry Dale. Slightly abridged.

should be delivered over those who are buried after falling in battle. To me, however, it would have appeared sufficient, that when men had shown themselves brave by deeds, their honors also should be displayed by deeds—as you now see in the case of this burial, prepared at the public expense—and not that the virtues of many should be periled in one individual for credit to be given him according as he expresses himself well or ill. For it is difficult to speak with propriety on a subject on which even the impression of one's truthfulness is with difficulty established.

Now with regard to our military achievements, by which each possession was gained, whether in any case it were ourselves, or our fathers, that repelled with spirit hostilities brought against us by barbarian or Greek; as I do not wish to enlarge on the subject before you who are well acquainted with it, I will pass them over. But by what a mode of life we attained to our power, and by what form of government and owing to what habits it became so great, I will explain these points first, and then proceed to the eulogy of these men; as I consider that on the present occasion they will not be inappropriately mentioned, and that it is profitable for the whole assembly, both citizens and strangers, to listen to them.

For we enjoy a form of government which does not copy the laws of our neighbors; but we are ourselves rather a pattern to others than imitators of them. In name, from its not being administered for the benefit of the few, but of the many, it is called a democracy; but with regard to its laws, all enjoy equality, as concerns their private differences; while with regard to public rank, according as each man has reputation for anything, he is preferred for public honors, not so much from consideration of party, as of merit; nor, again, on the ground of poverty, while he is able to do the state any good service, is he prevented by the obscurity of his position. We are liberal then in our public administration; and with regard to mutual jealousy of our daily pursuits, we are not angry with our neighbor, if he does anything to please himself; nor wear on our countenance offensive looks, which tho harmless, are yet unpleasant. While, however, in private matters we live together agreeably, in public matters, under the influence of fear, we most carefully abstain from transgression, through our obedience to those who are from time to time in office, and to the laws; especially such of them as are enacted for the benefit of the injured, and such as, tho unwritten, bring acknowledged disgrace [on those who break them].

Moreover, we have provided for our spirits the most numerous recreations from labors, by celebrating games and sacrifices through the whole year, and by maintaining elegant private establishments, of which the daily gratification drives away sadness. Owing to the greatness too of our city, everything from every land is imported into it; and it is our lot to reap with no more peculiar enjoyment the good things which are produced here, than those of the rest of the world likewise.

In the studies of war also we differ from our enemies in the following respects: We throw our city open to all, and never, by the expulsion of strangers, exclude anyone from either learning or observing things, by seeing which unconcealed any of our enemies might gain an advantage; for we trust not so much to preparations and stratagems, as to our own valor for daring deeds. Again, as to our modes of education, *they* aim at the acquisition of a manly character, by laborious training from their very youth; while *we*, tho living at our ease, no less boldly advance to meet equal dangers. As a proof of this, the Lacedæmonians never march against our country singly, but with all [their confederates] together: while we, generally speaking, have no difficulty in conquering in battle upon hostile ground those who are standing up in defense of their own. And no enemy ever yet encountered our whole united force, through our attending at the same time to our navy, and sending our troops by land on so many different services: but wherever they have engaged with any part of it, if they conquer only some of us, they boast that we were all routed by them; and if they are conquered, they say it was by all that they were beaten. And yet if with careless ease rather than with laborious practise, and with a courage which is the result not so much of laws as of natural disposition, we are willing to face danger, we have the advantage of not suffering beforehand from coming troubles, and of proving ourselves, when we are involved in them, no less bold than those who are always toiling; so that our country is worthy of admiration in these respects, and in others besides.

For we study taste with economy, and philosophy without effeminacy; and employ wealth rather for opportunity of action than for boastfulness of talking; while poverty is nothing disgraceful for a man to confess, but not to escape it by exertion is more disgraceful. Again, the same men can attend at the same time to domestic as well as to public affairs; and others, who are engaged with business, can still form a sufficient judgment on political questions. For we are the only people that consider the man who takes no part in these things, not as unofficious, but as useless; and we ourselves judge rightly of measures, at any rate, if we do not originate them; while we do not regard words as any hindrance to deeds, but rather [consider it a hindrance] not to have been previously instructed by word, before undertaking in deed what we have to do. For we have this characteristic also in a remarkable degree, that we are at the same time most daring and most calculating in what we take in hand, whereas to other men it is igno-

rance that brings daring, while calculation brings
fear.

In short, I say that both the whole city is a
school for Greece, and that, in my opinion, the
same individual would among us provide himself qualified for the most varied kinds of action, and with the most graceful versatility. And
that this is not mere vaunting language for the
occasion, so much as actual truth, the very power
of the state, which we have won by such habits,
affords a proof. For it is the only country at
the present time that, when brought to the test,
proves superior to its fame; and the only one
that neither gives to the enemy who has attacked
us any cause for indignation at being worsted
by such opponents, nor to him who is subject to
us room for finding fault, as not being ruled by
men who are worthy of empire. But we shall
be admired both by present and future generations as having exhibited our power with great
proofs, and by no means without evidence; and
as having no further need, either of Homer to
praise us or anyone else who might charm for
the moment by his verses, while the truth of the
facts would mar the idea formed of them; but
as having compelled every sea and land to become accessible to our daring, and everywhere
established everlasting records, whether of evil
or of good. It was for such a country then that
these men, nobly resolving not to have it taken
from them, fell fighting; and every one of their

survivors may well be willing to suffer in its behalf.

For this reason, indeed, it is that I have enlarged on the characteristics of the state; both to prove that the struggle is not for the same object in our case as in that of men who have none of these advantages in an equal degree; and at the same time clearly to establish by proofs [the truth of] the eulogy of those men over whom I am now speaking. And now the chief points of it have been mentioned; for with regard to the things for which I have commended the city, it was the virtues of these men, such as these, that adorned her with them; and few of the Greeks are there whose fame, like these men's, would appear but the just counterpoise of their deeds.

Again, the closing scene of these men appears to me to supply an illustration of human worth, whether as affording us the first information respecting it, or its final confirmation. For even in the case of men who have been in other respects of an inferior character, it is but fair for them to hold forth as a screen their military courage in their country's behalf; for, having wiped out their evil by their good, they did more service collectively, than harm by their individual offenses.

But of these men there was none that either was made a coward by his wealth, from preferring the continued enjoyment of it; or shrank from danger through a hope suggested by pov-

erty, namely, that he might yet escape it, and
grow rich; but conceiving that vengeance on
their foes was more to be desired than these objects, and at the same time regarding this as
the most glorious of hazards, they wished by
risking it to be avenged on their enemies, and
so to aim at procuring those advantages; committing to hope the uncertainty of success, but
resolving to trust to action, with regard to what
was visible to themselves; and in that action,
being minded rather to resist and die, than by
surrendering to escape, they fled from the shame
of [a discreditable] report, while they endured
the brunt of the battle with their bodies; and
after the shortest crisis, when at the very height
of their fortune, were taken away from their
glory rather than their fear.

Such did these men prove themselves, as became the character of their country. For you
that remain, you must pray that you may have
a more successful resolution, but must determine
not to have one less bold against your enemies;
not in word alone considering the benefit [of such
a spirit], (on which one might descant to you
at great length—tho you know it yourselves quite
as well—telling you how many advantages are
contained in repelling your foes) but rather
day by day beholding the power of the city as
it appears in fact, and growing enamored of it,
and reflecting, when you think it great that it
was by being bold, and knowing their duty, and
being alive to shame in action, that men acquired

these things; and because, if they ever failed in their attempt at anything, they did not on that account think it right to deprive their country also of their valor, but conferred upon her a most glorious joint-offering.

For while collectively they gave her their lives, individually they received that renown which never grows old, and the most distinguished tomb they could have; not so much that in which they are laid, as that in which their glory is left behind them, to be everlastingly recorded on every occasion for doing so, either by word or deed, that may from time to time present itself. For of illustrious men the whole earth is the sepulcher; and not only does the inscription upon columns in their own land point it out, but in that also which is not their own there dwells with every one an unwritten memorial of the heart, rather than of a material monument.

Vying then with these men in your turn, and deeming happiness to consist in freedom, and freedom in valor, do not think lightly of the hazards of war. For it is not the unfortunate, [and those] who have no hope of any good, that would with most reason be unsparing of their lives; but those who, while they live, still incur the risk of a change to the opposite condition, and to whom the difference would be the greatest, should they meet with any reverse. For more grievous, to a man of high spirit at least, is the misery which accompanies cowardice, than the unfelt death which comes upon him at once, in the time of his strength and of his hope for the common welfare.

Wherefore to the parents of the dead—as many of them as are here among you—I will not offer condolence, so much as consolation. For they know that they have been brought up subject to manifold misfortunes; but that happy is *their* lot who have gained the most glorious—death, as these have,—sorrow, as you have; and to whom life has been so exactly measured, that they were both happy in it, and died in [that happiness]. Difficult, indeed, I know it is to persuade you of this, with regard to those of whom you will often be reminded by the good fortune of others, in which you yourselves also once rejoiced; and sorrow is felt, not for the blessings of which one is bereft without full experience of them, but of that which one loses after becoming accustomed to it.

But you must bear up in the hope of other children, those of you whose age yet allows you to have them. For to yourselves individually those who are subsequently born will be a reason for your forgetting those who are no more; and to the state it will be beneficial in two ways, by its not being depopulated, and by the enjoyment of security; for it is not possible that those should offer any fair and just advice, who do not incur equal risk with their neighbors by having children at stake. Those of you, however, who are past that age, must consider that the longer period of your life during which you have been prosperous is so much gain, and that what remains will be a short one; and you must cheer yourselves with the fair fame of these [your lost ones]. For the love of honor is the only feeling that never grows old; and in the helplessness of age it is not the acquisition of gain, as some assert, that gives greatest pleasure, but the enjoyment of honor.

For those of you, on the other hand, who are sons or brothers of the dead, great, I see, will be the struggle of competition. For every one is accustomed to praise the man who is no more; and scarcely, tho even for an excess of worth, would you be esteemed, I do not say equal to them, but only slightly inferior. For the living are exposed to envy in their rivalry; but those who are in no one's way are honored with a good will free from all opposition. If, again, I must say anything on the subject of woman's excellence also, with reference to those of you who will now be in widowhood, I will express it all in a brief exhortation. Great will be your glory in not falling short of the natural character that belongs to you; and great is hers, who is least talked of among the men, either for good or evil.

I have now expressed *in word*, as the law required, what I had to say befitting the occasion; and, *in deed*, those who are here interred, have already received part of their honors, while, for the remaining part, the state will bring up their sons at the public expense, from this time to their manhood; thus offering both to these and to their posterity a beneficial reward for such contests; for where the greatest prizes for virtue are given, there also the most virtuous men are found amongst the citizens. And now, having finished your lamentations for your several relatives, depart.

III

IN DEFENSE OF HIMSELF[1]
(430 B.C.)

I HAD both expected the proofs of your anger against me, which have been exhibited (for I am aware of the causes of it), and have now convened an assembly for this purpose, that I may remind you [of what you have forgotten], and reprove you if in any respect you are wrong, either in being irritated against me or in succumbing to your misfortunes. For I consider that a state which in its public capacity is successful confers more benefit on individuals than one which is prosperous as regards its particular citizens, while collectively it comes to ruin. For tho a man is individually prosperous, yet if

---

[1] Delivered before an assembly in Athens called for the purpose, after violent criticism had been made of his influence in bringing on the Peloponnesian War. Reported by Thucydides. Translated by Henry Dale. Slightly abridged.

his country is ruined, he none the less shares in
its destruction; whereas, if he is unfortunate in
a country that is fortunate, he has a much better hope of escaping his dangers.

Since then a state is able to bear the misfortunes of individuals, while each individual is
unable to bear hers, how can it fail to be the
duty of all to support her, and not to act as *you*
are now doing, who, being panic-stricken by your
domestic afflictions, give up all thought of the
public safety, and are blaming both me who advised you to go to war, and yourselves who joined
in voting for it. And yet I, with whom you are
angry, am a man who deem myself second to
none in at once knowing what measures are required, and explaining them to others; a lover
too of my country, and superior to the influence
of money. For he who knows a thing that is
right, but does not explain it with clearness, is
no better than if he had never had a conception
of it; and he, again, who has both these requisites,
but is ill-affected towards his country, would not
so well speak for her interest. And even if this
qualification be added to the others, while he is
influenced by regard for money, all of them together would be sacrificed for this one consideration. So that if you were persuaded by me to
go to war, because you thought that I possessed
these qualities even in a moderate degree more
than other men, I can not now fairly be charged
with injuring you, at any rate.

For those indeed to go to war, who, while suc-

cessful in other things, have had a choice in the
matter allowed them, it is great folly. But if
[in our case] it were necessary, either immediately to submit to our neighbors, if we made concessions, or to preserve our independence by running a great risk, then he who shrank from the
risk is more reprehensible than he who faced it.
For my part then, I am the same that I ever
was, and do not depart from my opinion; but
you are changing, since it happens that you
were persuaded [to go to war] while unscathed,
but repent of it now you are suffering: and that
my advice appears wrong through the weakness
of your resolution; because pain is now in possession of each man's feeling, while the certainty
of the benefit is as yet hidden from all: and a
great reverse having befallen you, and that sud-
denly, your mind is too prostrated to persevere
in your determinations.

But with regard to your trouble in the war,
lest you should fear that it may prove great, and
we may still be none the more successful, let
those arguments suffice you, with which on many
other occasions I have proved the error of your
suspicions respecting it. At the same time, I
will also lay before you the following advantage,
which yourselves do not appear ever yet to have
thought of as belonging to you, respecting the
greatness of your empire, and which I never
urged in my former speeches; nor would I even
now, as it has rather too boastful an air, if I
did not see you unreasonably cast down. You

think then that you only bear rule over your own subject allies; but I declare to you that of the two parts of the world open for man's use, the land and the sea, of the whole of the one you are most absolute masters, both as far as you avail yourselves of it now, and if you should wish to do so still further; and there is no power, neither the king nor any nation besides at the present day, that can prevent your sailing [where you please] with your present naval resources.

This power then evidently is far from being merely on a level with the benefits of your houses and lands, which you think so much to be deprived of: nor is it right for you to grieve about them, but rather to hold them cheap, considering them, in comparison with this as a mere garden-plot and embellishment of a rich man's estate. You should know, too, that liberty, provided we devote ourselves to *that*, and preserve it, will easily recover these losses; whereas those who have once submitted to others find even their greatest gains diminish. Nor should you show yourselves inferior in both respects to your fathers, who with labor, and not by inheritance from others, acquired these possessions, and moreover kept them and bequeathed them to us; for it is more disgraceful to be deprived of a thing when we have got it, than to fail in getting it. On the contrary, you should meet your enemies, not only with spirit, but also with a spirit of contempt. For *confidence* is produced even by lucky ignorance, ay, even in a coward; but *contempt* is the feeling of the man who trusts that he is superior to his adversaries in counsel also, which is our case. And ability, with a high spirit, renders more sure the daring which arises from equal fortune; and does not so much trust to mere hope, whose strength mainly displays itself in difficulties; but rather to a judgment grounded upon present realities, whose anticipations may be more relied upon.

It is but fair, too, that you should sustain the dignity of the state derived from its sovereignty, on which you all pride yourselves; and that either you should not shrink from its labors, or else should lay no claim to its honors either. Nor should you suppose that you are struggling to escape one evil only, slavery instead of freedom; but to avoid loss of dominion also, and danger from the animosities which you have incurred in your exercise of that dominion. And from this it is no longer possible for you to retire; if through fear at the present time any one is for so playing the honest man in quiet. For you now hold it as a tyranny, which it seems wrong to have assumed, but dangerous to give up. And men with these views would very quickly ruin the state, whether they persuaded others [to adopt the same], or even lived anywhere independently by themselves; for quietness is not a safe principle, unless ranged with activity; nor is it for the interest of a sovereign state, but of a subject one, that it may live in safe slavery.

Do you then neither be seduced by such citizens, nor be angry with me, whom yourselves also joined in voting for war, tho the enemy has invaded our country, and done what it was natural that he should do, if you would not submit; and tho, besides what we looked for, this disease also has come upon us—the only thing, indeed, of all that has happened beyond our expectations. And it is through this, I well know, that in some degree I am still more the object of your displeasure; yet not with justice unless you will also give me the credit when you meet with any success beyond your calculation. The evils then which are sent by heaven, you must bear perforce; those which are inflicted by your enemies, with courage: for such was formerly the custom of this country, and let it not now meet with a check in your case.

But consider that it has the greatest name in all the world from not yielding to misfortunes, and from expending in war more lives and labors than any other state; and that it has now the greatest power that ever existed up to the present time; the memory of which, even should we now at length give way (for everything is naturally liable to decrease), will be left to posterity for ever, namely, that we had dominion over more Greeks than any other Greek state ever had; and held out in the greatest wars against them, both collectively and singly; and inhabited a city better provided with all things than any other, and greater. And yet your quiet man would find fault with these things; but the man who has himself a wish to achieve something, will emulate them; while whoever does not possess them will envy them.

But to be hated and offensive for the time present has been the lot of all who have ever presumed to rule over others; that man, however, takes wise counsel, who incurs envy for the greatest things. For odium does not last long; but present splendor and future glory are handed down to perpetual memory. Do you then, providing both for your future honor, and for your immediate escape from disgrace, secure both objects by your present spirit: and neither send any heralds to the Lacedæmonians, nor show that you are weighed down by your present troubles; for such as in feeling are least annoyed at their misfortunes, while in action they most courageously resist them, these, both of states and of individuals, are the best.

CLEON

ON THE PUNISHMENT OF THE MYTILENEANS

(427 B.C.)

Born after 500 B.C., died in 422; usually classed as a demagog; came into prominence in 429 as an opponent of Pericles; violently opposed Nicias; in 425 placed in charge of operations against Sphæteria, serving with Demosthenes; in 422 defeated and slain in battle.

On many other occasions before this have I been convinced that a democracy is incapable of maintaining dominion over others, and I am so more than ever from your present change of purpose respecting the Mytilenæans. For owing to your daily freedom from fear, and from plotting against each other, you entertain the same views toward your allies also. And you do not reflect, in whatever case you may either have made a mistake through being persuaded by their words, or may have given way to pity, that you show such weakness to your own peril, and at the same time too gain no gratitude from your allies; not considering that it is a tyrannical dominion which you hold, and over men who are plotting against you, and involuntarily subject to you; and who obey you not from any favors you confer on them to your own hurt,

---

¹ Delivered in Athens before the Assembly, 427 B.C. Reported by Thucydides. Translated by Henry Dale. Slightly abridged.

but from the fact of your being superior to them through your power, rather than their good feeling.

But of all things, it is the most fearful, if nothing of what we have resolved is to be steadfast; and if we are not convinced that a state with inferior laws which are unchanged is better than one with good ones which are not authoritative; that homely wit with moderation is more useful than cleverness with intemperance; and that the duller class of men, compared with the more talented, generally speaking, manage public affairs better. For the latter wish to appear wiser than the laws, and to overrule what is ever spoken for the public good—thinking that they could not show their wisdom in more important matters—and by such means they generally ruin their country. But the former, distrusting their own talent, deign to be less learned than the laws, and less able than to find fault with the words of one who has spoken well; and being judges on fair terms, rather than rivals for a prize, they are more commonly right in their views. So then ought *we* also to do, and not to advise your people contrary to our real opinion, urged on by cleverness and rivalry of talent.

I, then, continue of the same opinion; and am astonished at those who have proposed to discuss a second time the case of the Mytileneans, and caused in it a delay of time, which is all for the advantage of the guilty (for so the sufferer proceeds against the offender with his anger less keen; whereas when retribution treads most closely on the heels of suffering, it best matches it in wreaking vengeance). I wonder, too, who will be the man to maintain the opposite opinion, and to pretend to show that the injuries done by the Mytileneans are beneficial to us, and that our misfortunes are losses to our allies. It is evident that either trusting to his eloquence he would strive to prove, in opposition to us, that what we consider most certain has not been ascertained; or, urged on by the hope of gain, will endeavor to lead us away by an elaborate display of specious language. But in such contests as these the state gives the prizes to others, and takes only the dangers itself. And it is you who are to blame for it, through unwisely instituting these contests; inasmuch as you are accustomed to attend to speeches like spectators [in a theater], and to facts like mere listeners [to what others tell you]; with regard to things future, judging of their possibility from those who have spoken cleverly about them; and with regard to things which have already occurred, not taking what has been done as more creditable from your having seen it, than what has been only heard from those who in words have delivered a clever invective. And so you are the best men to be imposed on with novelty of argument, and to be unwilling to follow up what has been approved by you; being slaves to every new paradox, and despisers of what is ordinary. Each of you wishes, above all, to be able to speak himself; but if that is not possible, in rivalry of those who so speak, you strive not to appear to have followed his sentiments at second-hand; but when he has said any thing cleverly, you would fain appear to have anticipated its expression by your applause, and are eager to catch beforehand what is said, and at the same time slow to forsee the consequences of it.

Wishing then to call you off from this course, I declare to you that the Mytileneans have injured you more than any one state ever did. For I can make allowance for men who have revolted because they could not endure your government, or because they were compelled by their enemies. But for those who inhabited an island with fortifications, and had only to fear our enemies by sea, on which element, too, they were themselves not unprotected against them by a fleet of triremes, and who lived independent, and were honored in the highest degree by us, and then treated us in this way; what else did those men do than deliberately devise our ruin, and rise up against us, rather than revolt from us (revolt, at least, is the part of those who are subject to some violent treatment), and seek to ruin us by siding with our bitterest enemies? Yet surely that is more intolerable than if they waged war against you by themselves for the acquisition of power.

But success is wont to make those states insolent to which it comes most unexpected and with the shortest notice; whereas the good fortune which is according to men's calculation is generally more steady than when it comes beyond their expectation; and, so to say, they more easily drive off adversity than they preserve prosperity. The Mytileneans then ought all along to have been honored by us on the same footing as the rest, and in that case they would not have come to such a pitch of insolence; for in other instances, as well as theirs, man is naturally inclined to despise those who court him, and to respect those who do not stoop to him. But let them even now be punished as their crimes deserve; and let not the guilt attach to the aristocracy, while you acquit the commons. For at any rate they all alike attacked *you;* since they might have come over to us, and so have been now in possession of their city again. Thinking, however, the chance they ran with the aristocracy to be the safer, they joined them in revolting.

And now consider; if you attach the same penalties to those of the allies who were compelled by their enemies to revolt, and to those who did it voluntarily, which of them, think you, will not revolt on any slight pretext, whether he either gains his liberation, if he succeed, or incurs no extreme suffering, if he fail? And so we shall presently have to risk both our money and our lives against each separate state.

You ought not therefore to hold out any hope,

either relying on oratory or purchased with money, of their receiving allowance for having erred through human infirmity. For they did not involuntarily hurt you, but wittingly plotted against you; and it is only what is involuntary that can claim allowance. I, then, both on that first occasion [so advised you], and now contend that you should not rescind your former resolutions, nor err through three things, the most inexpedient for empire, namely, pity, delight in oratory, and lenity. For pity is property felt toward those of a kindred temper, and not toward those who will not feel it in return, but are of necessity our enemies for ever. And the orators who delight us with their language will have a field in other subjects of less importance, instead of one in which the state, after being a little pleased, will pay a great penalty; while they themselves from their good speaking will receive good treatment in return. And lenity is shown to those who will be well-disposed in future, rather than to those who remain just what they were, and not at all less hostile.

To sum up in one word, if you are persuaded by me, you will do what is just toward the Mytileneans, and at the same time expedient; but if you decide otherwise, you will not oblige *them*, but will rather pass sentence upon *yourselves*. For if they were right in revolting, you cannot properly maintain your empire. If, however, you determine to do so, even tho it is not proper, you must also, overlooking what is right, punish these men from regard to expediency, or else give up your empire, and act the honest man without danger. Resolve, then, to requite them with the same penalty; and not to show yourselves, in escaping their designs, more insensible than those who formed them against you; considering what they would probably have done, if they had prevailed over you; especially, as they were the first to begin the wrong. For it is those who do ill to any one without reason, that persecute him most bitterly, nay, even to the death, from suspicion of the danger of their enemy's being spared; since he who has suffered evil without any necessity [but by provoking it himself] is more bitter, if he escape, than one who was an enemy on equal terms.

Be not therefore traitors to your own cause; but bringing yourselves in feeling as near as possible to the actual state of suffering, and reflecting how you would in that case have valued their subjection above everything, now pay them back in return, not indulging in weakness at the present moment, nor forgetting the danger which once hung over you. Punish these men, I say, as they deserve; and give a striking example to the rest of your allies, that whoever revolts will pay the penalty for it with his life. For if they know this, you will less freuently have to neglect your enemies, while you are fighting with your own confederates.

ALCIBIADES

I

IN SUPPORT OF THE ATHENIAN EXPEDITION TO SICILY [1]

(414 B.C.)

Born in Athens in 450 B.C., died in 404; at his suggestion Athens undertook the Sicilian expedition, out of which came the military career of Alcibiades, during which he was assassinated in Phrygia, pierced by a volley of arrows.

It is both befitting, Athenians, for me, more than others, to enjoy command (for with this topic must I commence my speech, since Cleon has attacked me upon it), and at the same time, I deem myself worthy of it. For those things about which I am so assailed with clamor, confer honor on my ancestors and myself, and benefit on my country at the same time. For the Greeks considered our state to be greater than they had ever done, even beyond its actual power, through the splendor of my display as its deputy to the Olympic games (whereas they hoped before that it had been exhausted by the war); inasmuch as I entered seven chariots—a number which no private individual had ever yet entered—and gained the first prize, and was second and fourth, and provided everything else in a style worthy of my victory. For according

[1] Delivered in Athens as reported by Thucydides. Translated by Henry Dale.

to the usual view of them, such things are a subject of honor; while, from the practise of them, an idea of power is also formed. And again, whatever distinction I gain at home by my exhibitions of choruses, or in any other way, it is naturally envied by my fellow citizens, but for foreigners this too has an appearance of power. And this is no useless folly, when a man benefits at his own costs, not himself only, but his country also.

Nor is it unfair for one who prides himself on his own prosperity, to refuse to be on an equality with the mass; since in the same way he who is unfortunate shares his calamities with no one else. But as we are not courted when in adversity, by the same rule let a man also submit to be slighted by the prosperous; or let him treat the unfortunate as on an equal footing [when he is in prosperity], and so claim the like treatment in return [when he is himself in adversity]. I know, however, that men in such circumstances, and all who ever surpassed others in splendor of any kind, though disliked in their own lifetime, most of all in their dealings with their equals, and then with the rest of the world also, have yet left to some of those who came after them a desire to claim connection with them, even where there were no grounds for it; and a subject for glorying to the country they belonged to, not as for aliens, or offenders, but as for countrymen, who had achieved glorious things. And in my case, who aim at such things, and am therefore in private assailed with clamor, consider, with regard to public affairs, whether I administer them in a manner inferior to any one else, or not. For having united the most powerful states of the Peloponnese, without any great danger or expense to you, I brought the Lacedæmonians to a single day's struggle for their all at Mantinea; in consequence of which, altho they were victorious in the battle, they do not ever now feel any firm confidence in themselves.

In this way, then, did my youth and preternatural folly, as it is thought, deal with the power of the Peloponnesians by means of suitable arguments; and, gaining credit by my vehemence, obtained their assent. And now too be not afraid of it; but while I am still in the flower of it, and Nicias appears fortunate, avail yourselves fully of the services of each of us. And with regard to the expedition to Sicily, change not your determination from an idea that it would be undertaken against a great power. For it is only with a mixed rabble that its cities are populous; and they easily admit changes in their government, and adopt new ones. And for this reason no one is furnished, as though in behalf of his own country, either with arms for the person, or with ordinary resources, as regards the country; but whatever each one thinks that he can get from the people, either by persuading them through his oratory, or by factious measures, and will so find a home in another land, in case of his not being successful, with that he provides himself. It is not likely, then, that a populace of such a character should either listen to any counsel with one heart, or apply themselves to action in common; but they would severally side with whatever was said to please them; especially if they are torn by factions, as we hear.

Again, with regard to heavy-armed troops, neither have the Siceliots so many as are boasted of, nor did the rest of the Greeks prove so numerous as they severally reckoned themselves; but Greece had very much misstated them, and was with difficulty equipped with them in sufficient numbers on the outbreak of this war. The states in those parts, then, from what I learn by report, are of this character, and still more easy to deal with—for we shall have many barbarians, who from hatred of the Syracusans will join us in attacking them—and those here will not prove an obstacle, if you take a right view of the matter. For our fathers had these very men, whom they say you would leave behind you in hostility when sailing there, and the Mede beside, as their enemies; and still they won their empire; tho strong in nothing else but the superiority of their fleet. And as things stand now, never yet were the Peloponnesians more hopeless with regard to us; and even if they are ever so confident, for invading our country indeed they are strong enough, even tho we do not undertake the expedition; but with their naval force they cannot hurt us [tho we do not undertake it], for we have a fleet left behind that is a match for them.

On what reasonable argument, then, could we ourselves shrink from it; or on what plea addressed to our allies there could we refuse to succor them? For since we have entered into league with them, we ought to assist them, and not to object that they too have not assisted us. For we united them with us, not that they might come here to help us in their turn, but that by annoying our enemies there they might prevent their coming here to attack us. And it is in this way that empire has been won, both by us and by all others who have enjoyed it; I mean, by readily taking part with those barbarians or Greeks who from time to time called them to their aid; since if all should remain quiet, or nicely choose whom they ought to assist; we should make but slight additions to it, but should rather run a risk of losing even what it now is. For men do not only defend themselves against a superior when he has attacked them, but also strike the first blow, to prevent his attacking them. And it is not possible for us to portion out exactly how far we wish to hold dominion; but since we are in our present position, we must form designs against some, and not give up others; because we should be subjected to the rule of another party, if we did not ourselves rule over others. Nor must you take the same view of quiet as the rest of the world, unless you will also receive fresh institutions assimilating to theirs. Considering, then, that we shall rather aggrandize our possessions here, if we go in quest of those there, let us make the expedition; that we may both prostrate the pride of the Peloponnesians, by being seen, regardless of present peace, to sail even against Sicily; and at the same time, by either ruling, as we most probably shall, over the whole of Greece, through being joined by those there, or at any rate by injuring the Syracusans, by which both ourselves and our allies will be benefited.

And as for security, whether for remaining there, in case of any success, or for returning, our fleet will provide us with it; for by sea we shall be superior to all the Siceliots put together. And let not the non-interfering policy which Nicias recommends in his speeches, nor his setting the young against the old, divert you from your purpose; but acting in your usual order, just as our fathers, by consulting young with old, raised the state to its present height, do ye now too, in the same manner, endeavor to advance it; being convinced that youth and old age can do nothing without each other; but that the period of levity, and of mid-age, and of extreme preciseness, will have most power when joined together; and that the state, if it remain quiet, will be worn out on itself, like anything else, and its skill in everything grow dull; while by entering into contest it will continually gain fresh experience, and will find self-defense habitual to it, not in word, but rather in deed. My

decided opinion then is, that I think a state of
no inactive character would most quickly be
ruined by a change to inactivity; and that those
men live most securely, who regulate their affairs
in accordance with their existing habits and institutions, even though they may be of an inferior character, with the least variation.

II

TO THE SPARTANS[1]

(413 B.C.)

AND now I beg that I may not be the worse
thought of by any among you, because I am now
strenuously attacking my country with its bitterest enemies, tho I formerly had a reputation
for patriotism; and that my words may not be
suspected on the score of an exile's forwardness.
For tho I am an exile, as regards the villainy of
those who banished me, I am not one, as regards
assistance to you, if you will be persuaded by
me; and the party hostile to me was, not you,
who only hurt your foes, but rather they who
compelled their friends to become their foes.
My patriotism, too, I keep not at a time when

---

[1] Delivered in Sparta in 413 B.C. Alcibiades, on being recalled
from Sicily to stand trial at Athens, had gone to Sparta, where he
prevailed upon its people to assist Syracuse in the war with Athens.
Reported by Thucydides. Translated by Henry Dale.

I am being wronged, but only while I enjoyed my civil rights in security. Nor do I consider myself to be going against what is still my country, but much rather to be recovering that country which is mine no more. And the patriot, in the true sense, is not that man who, when he has unjustly lost his country, abstains from aggression upon it, but he who, because of his longing for it, endeavors by all means to regain it. Thus, as far as I am concerned, I beg you, Lacedæmonians, fearlessly to command my services, both for danger and trouble of every kind; knowing that argument which is advanced by all, namely, that if as your enemy I did you very great harm, I might also as your friend do you great service; inasmuch as I *know* the plans of the Athenians, while I only *guessed* yours. I beg, too, that on your own part also, being convinced that you are consulting about your greatest interests, you will not shrink from the expedition both against Sicily and Attica; that by joining them with a small part of your forces, you may at once preserve the great states in Sicily, and overthrow the present and future power of the Athenians; and may afterwards live in security yourselves, and enjoy a voluntary supremacy over the whole of Greece, resting not on force but on affection.

NICIAS

AGAINST THE SICILIAN EXPEDITION [1]
(414 B.C.)

As a general, successful against the Spartans; the peace of 421 B.C.
named after him; one of the commanders of the expedition against
Sicily which he had strongly opposed; won several battles, but was
defeated in 413 and put to death.

THIS assembly was, it is true, convened to consider the subject of our preparations, namely, in
what way we ought to make the expedition to
Sicily. My opinion, however, is, that we ought
still to consider this very point, whether it be
better to send out our ships; and not on such
slight deliberation on matters of great moment,
at the instigation of aliens, to take upon ourselves a war with which we have nothing to do.
And yet I, for my own part, receive honor from
such a policy, and have less fear than others for
my own personal safety (tho I consider that
man to be an equally good citizen who takes some
forethought both for his person and his property;
for such a man would, for his own sake, be most
desirous that his country also should prosper);
nevertheless, neither aforetime have I ever
spoken contrary to my convictions, for the sake
of being honored above others, nor will I now,
but as I think best, so will I speak. And tho

[1] Delivered before the Assembly at Athens. Reported by Thucydides. Translated by Henry Dale. One paragraph omitted.

against your inclinations my words would be powerless, should I advise you to keep what you have, and not expose your present possessions to danger for things which are uncertain and future; yet that neither are you timely in your haste, nor the objects of your ambition easy to attain, on these points I will give you instruction.

I say then, that you wish, tho leaving many enemies behind you here, to bring hither fresh ones besides, by sailing there. And you fancy, perhaps, that the treaty that has been made by you affords some ground of confidence. But tho as long as you remain quiet, that will, indeed, be a treaty—in name (for this condition have certain persons here and among your enemies brought it by their intrigues), yet if we are ever defeated with any considerable force, those who hate us will quickly make an attack upon us; seeing, in the first place, that the arrangement was made of necessity by them, under circumstances of disaster, and of greater discredit to them than to us; and, secondly, that in this very arrangement we have many subjects open to debate. There are some, too, who have not yet acceded even to this composition, such as it is, and those not the least powerful states; but some of them are at war with us downright, and, in the case of others, because the Lacedæmonians remain quiet at present, they too are restrained by truces from one ten days to another. But probably, if they should find our power divided (which we are now so anxious to bring about), they would with all their might attack us, in conjunction with the Siceliots, whose alliance they would in time past have valued most highly.

Every one therefore ought to look to this, and not presume to run risks with a state so unsettled, and to grasp at another empire before we have secured the one we have; seeing that the Chalcidians Thraceward, tho they have revolted from us so many years, are still unsubdued; and there are some others on the different coasts of the mainland who yield us but a doubtful obedience. And so we are quick to succor the Segestans, who are our allies, forsooth, as being injured; but on those by whose revolt we have ourselves long ago been injured, we still defer to avenge ourselves.

And yet the latter, if subdued, might be kept in subjection by us; but the former, even if we conquered them, we should hardly be able to govern, so far off and so numerous as they are. But it is folly to go against men whom we could not keep under, if we conquered them; while, if we did not succeed in the attempt, we should not be in the same position as we were before making it. Again, regarding the present condition of the Siceliots, they appear to me even still less likely to be formidable to us, if the Syracusans should have dominion over them; that supposition with which the Segestans especially try to frighten us. For at present they might, perhaps, come hither as separate states, to oblige the Lacedæmonians; but in the other case, it is not likely that they should undertake the expedition, empire against empire; for in the same manner as they, in conjunction with the Lacedæmonians, had taken away ours, it is probable that they would have their own taken away by the same Peloponnesians, and by the same principle.

And the Greeks in those parts would be most in awe of us, if we did not go there at all; and next to that, if after making a demonstration of our power we retired in a short time; but if we should meet with any reverse, they would very quickly despise us, and attack us in concert with our enemies here. For we all know that what is farthest off is most admired, and what gives the least room for having its fame tested. And this has at present been your case, Athenians, with reference to the Lacedæmonians and their allies; from having, contrary to your expectation, gained the advantage over them (comparing your present position with the fears you at first entertained), you have despised them, and are now desiring the conquest of Sicily. You ought not, however, to be elated through the misfortunes of your adversaries, but then only to feel confident when you have mastered their spirits; nor should you think that the Lacedæmonians are doing aught but considering, in consequence of their disgrace, in what way they may even now, if possible, overthrow us, and bring their own discredit to a happy termination; especially as they have studied a reputation for bravery, as a thing of the greatest importance, and for the greatest length of time. So that our great struggle will be, if we are wise, not for the Segestans in Sicily, men who are barbarians, but that we may vigorously guard against a state which is plotting against us by the spread of oligarchical principles.

I am alarmed, indeed, when I see such characters sitting here at present by the side of that same individual, in compliance with his bidding; and in return I bid the older men—whichever of them may have one of those characters sitting by him—not to be put down through shame, in order to avoid being thought a coward if he should not vote for going to war; nor, as their opponents themselves might feel, to be madly enamored of what they do not possess; being convinced that in very few things do men succeed through desire, but in very many through forethought; but in behalf of their country, as exposing itself to the greatest danger it has ever done, to give their support to the opposite side, and vote that the Siceliots keep the same boundaries with respect to us as at present—boundaries with which no one can find fault—namely, the Ionian Sea, if one sail along shore; and the Sicilian, if one cross the open deep; and that while they enjoy their own possessions, they shall also settle their own quarrels; and that we tell the Segestans in particular, that since they went to war with the Selinuntines in the first instance without consulting the Athenians, they may also make peace with them by themselves; and that we do not in future make alliance, as we have been accustomed, with men whom we shall assist when they are unfortunate, and when we ask assistance ourselves, shall not obtain it.

And do you, Prytanis, if you think it your duty to care for the state, and if you wish to show yourself a good citizen, put this to the vote, and take a second time the opinion of the Athenians; reflecting, if you feel afraid to move the question again, that the violation of the law would not, with so many abettors, involve any guilt; but that you would be acting as a physician to the state, when it had taken bad counsel; and that good government consists in this,—for a man to do his country as much good as possible, or, at least, to do it voluntarily no harm.

HERMOCRATES

ON THE UNION OF SICILY AGAINST INVADERS [1]

(416 B.C.)

Born in 460 B.C., died in 407; promoted the union of the Sicilian cities which made possible the defeat of Athens in 413; and in 412 went to Asia Minor, where he was successful for a time, but then lost a battle, was removed from command and sent into exile; fought against Carthage; died while attempting to reinstate himself in Syracuse.

IT is not because I am of a city that is either the least powerful, or the most distressed by hostilities that I shall address you, Sicilians, but in order publicly to state what appears to me the best policy for the whole of Sicily. And now with regard to war, to prove that it is a disastrous thing, why need one particularize all the evil involved in it, and so make a long speech before those who are acquainted with it? For no one is either driven to engage in it through ignorance, or deterred from it by fear, should he think that he will gain any advantage; but it is the lot of the former to imagine the gains greater than the dangers; and the latter will face the perils rather than put up with any present loss. But if both should happen to be thus acting unseasonably, exhortations to peace would be useful. And this would be most serviceable to us

---

[1] Delivered in Syracuse before the Assembly. Reported by Thucydides. Translated by Henry Dale.

too at the present time, if we did but believe it. For it was surely with a purpose of well securing our own several interests that we both went to war at first, and are endeavoring by means of conference to come to terms again with each other; and if each one should not succeed in going away with what is fair, we shall proceed to hostilities again.

We should be convinced, however, that it is not for our own separate interests alone, if we are wise, that this congress will be held; but to consider whether we shall be able any longer to save the whole of Sicily, which, as I conceive, is the object of the machinations of the Athenians. And we should regard that people as much more compulsory mediators in such case than my words; who, possessing as they do the greatest power of all the Greeks, are watching our blunders, being here with a few ships; and under the legitimate name of alliance are speciously bringing to a profitable conclusion their natural hostility to us. For if we go to war, and call them in to our aid, men who of their own accord turn their arms even upon such as do not call them in; and if we injure ourselves by means of our own resources, and at the same time pave the way for their dominion; it is probable that when they observe us worn out, they will come hereafter with a great force, and endeavor to bring all these states into subjection to them.

And yet we ought, if we are wise, to aim at acquiring for our own respective countries what does not belong to them, rather than at diminishing what they already have, both in calling in allies and incurring fresh dangers; and to consider that faction is most ruinous to states, and particularly to Sicily, the inhabitants of which are all being plotted against, while we are at variance city with city. Knowing this then, we ought to make peace, individual with individual, and state with state, and to make a common effort to save the whole of Sicily; and the thought should be entertained by no one, that tho the Dorian part of us are enemies of the Athenians, the Chalcidian race is secured by its Ionian connection. For they are not attacking our nations, because they are different, and from their hatred of one of them; but from coveting the good things of Sicily, which we possess in common. And this they have now shown upon the invitation of the Chalcidian race; for to those who had never yet assisted them on the ground of their alliance, they themselves with forwardness answered their claim, beyond the letter of the compact.

With regard to the Athenians then, so great is found to be the benefit of our taking good advice. And with regard to peace, which is acknowledged by all to be a most excellent thing, how can it fail to be incumbent on us to conclude it among ourselves? Or do you think, that whatever good thing, or the contrary, anyone has, quiet would not more effectually than war put a stop to the latter, and help to preserve the former; and that peace has not the less hazardous honors and splendors? with all other topics which one might discuss in many words, on such a subject as war. Considering then these things, you ought not to disregard what I say, but should rather provide each for your own safety in compliance with it. And if any one think that he shall certainly gain some advantage, either by right or might, let him not be annoyed by failure through the unexpected result; knowing that many men ere now, both while pursuing with vengeance those who have wronged them, and hoping, in other instances, to win an advantage by greater power, in the one case, so far from avenging themselves, have not even saved themselves; and in the other, instead of gaining more, have happened also to lose what they had. For vengeance is not necessarily successful, because a man is injured; nor is strength sure, because it is sanguine. But the incalculable nature of the future prevails to the greatest possible degree; and tho the most deceptive of all things, still proves the most useful; for because we are equally afraid, we are more cautious in attacking one another.

And now, on account of our indefinite fear of this unknown future, and our immediate dread of the Athenians' presence, being alarmed on both these grounds, and thinking, with regard to any failure in our ideas of what we severally thought to achieve, that these obstacles are a sufficient bar to their fulfilment, let us send away from the country the enemy that is among us, and ourselves make peace forever, if possible; but if not that, let us make a treaty for the longest term we can, and put off our private differences to a future period. In a word, let us be convinced that by following my advice we shall each have a free city, from which we shall, as our own masters, make an equally good return to him who treats us either well or ill; but if, through not following it, we are subject to others, then, not speak of avenging ourselves on any one, we necessarily become, even if most fortunate, friends to our greatest enemies, and at variance with those with whom we ought not to be so.

And for myself, altho, as I said at the beginning of my speech, I represent a most powerful city, and am more likely to attack another than to defend myself, yet I think it right to provide against these things, and to make concessions; and not so to injure my enemies as to incur greater damage myself; nor through a foolish animosity to think that I have absolute sway alike over my own plans and over fortune, which I can not control; but to give way, as far as is reasonable. And I call on you all, of your own free will, to act in the same manner as myself, and not to be compelled to do it by your enemies. For there is no disgrace in connections giving way to connections, whether a Dorian to a Dorian, or a Chalcidian to those of the same race; in a word, all of us who are neighbors, and live together in one country, and that an island, and are called by the one name of Sicilians. For we shall go to war again, I suppose, when it may so happen, and come to terms again among ourselves by means of general conferences; but to foreign invaders we shall always, if we are wise, offer united resistance, inasmuch as by our separate losses we are collectively endangered; and we shall never in future call in any allies or mediators. For by acting thus we shall at the present time avoid depriving Sicily of two blessings—riddance both of the Athenians and of civil war—and shall in future enjoy it by ourselves in freedom, and less exposed to the machinations of others.

LYSIAS

AGAINST ERATOSTHENES[1]
(403 B.C.)

Born about 440 B.C., died in 380; fled from the Thirty Tyrants in 404 after they had put his brother to death; returned to Athens after the restoration of the Democracy, and won great reputation as an orator, but only 34 of his 160 known speeches have survived.

IT is an easy matter, O Athenians, to begin this accusation. But to end it without doing injustice to the cause will be attended with no small difficulty. For the crimes of Eratosthenes are not only too atrocious to describe, but too many to enumerate. No exaggeration can exceed, and within the time assigned for this discourse it is impossible fully to represent them. This trial, too, is attended with another singularity. In other causes it is usual to ask the accusers: "What is your resentment against the defendants?" But here you must ask the defendant: "What was your resentment against your country? What malice did you bear your fellow citizens? Why did you rage with unbridled fury against the state itself?"

The time has now indeed come, Athenians, when, insensible to pity and tenderness, you must be armed with just severity against Eratos-

---

[1] Delivered in Athens in 403 B.C., and "the most splendid of his extant speeches," says R. C. Jebb. Eratosthenes, as one of the Tyrants, was responsible for the death of the brother of Lysias. Abridged.

thenes and his associates. What avails it to have conquered them in the field, if you be overcome by them in your councils? Do not show them more favor for what they boast they will perform, than resentment for what they have already committed. Nor, after having been at so much pains to become masters of their persons, allow them to escape without suffering that punishment which you once sought to inflict; but prove yourselves worthy of that good fortune which has given you power over your enemies.

The contest is very unequal between Eratosthenes and you. Formerly he was both judge and accuser; but we, even while we accuse, must at the same time make our defense. Those who were innocent he put to death without trial. To those who are guilty we allow the benefit of law, even tho no adequate punishment can ever be inflicted. For should we sacrifice them and their children, would this compensate for the murder of your fathers, your sons, and your brothers? Should we deprive them of their property, would this indemnify the individuals whom they have beggared, or the state which they have plundered? Tho they can not suffer a punishment adequate to their demerit, they ought not, surely, on this account, to escape. Yet how matchless is the effrontery of Eratosthenes, who, being now judged by the very persons whom he formerly injured, still ventures to make his defense before the witnesses of his crimes? What can show more evidently the contempt in which he holds you, or the confidence which he reposes in others?

Let me now conclude with laying before you the miseries to which you were reduced, that you may see the necessity of taking punishment on the authors of them. And first, you who remained in the city, consider the severity of their government. You were reduced to such a situation as to be forced to carry on a war, in which, if you were conquered, you partook indeed of the same liberty with the conquerers; but if you proved victorious, you remained under the slavery of your magistrates. As to you of the Piræus, you will remember that tho you never lost your arms in the battles which you fought, yet you suffered by these men what your foreign enemies could never accomplish, and at home, in times of peace, were disarmed by your fellow citizens. By them you were banished from the country left you by your fathers. Their rage, knowing no abatement, pursued you abroad, and drove you from one territory to another. Recall the cruel indignities which you suffered; how you were dragged from the tribunal and the altars; how no place, however sacred, could shelter you against their violence. Others, torn from their wives, their children, their parents, after putting an end to their miserable lives, were deprived of funeral rites; for these tyrants imagined their government so firmly established that even the vengeance of the gods was unable to shake it.

But it is impossible for one, or in the course of one trial, to enumerate the means which were employed to undermine the power of this state, the arsenals which were demolished, the temples sold or profaned, the citizens banished or murdered, and those whose dead bodies were impiously left uninterred. Those citizens now watch your decree, uncertain whether you will prove accomplices of their death or avengers of their murder. I shall desist from any further accusations. You have heard, you have seen, you have experienced. Decide then!

SOCRATES

I

IN HIS OWN DEFENSE[1]

(399 B.C.)

Born about 470 B.C., died in 399; for a time followed his father's art as a sculptor; served in three campaigns; President of the Pyrtanes in 406 and opposed the Thirty Tyrants; his philosophical precepts, as those of the wisest man of his time, known to us only in the writings of his disciple, Plato.

I KNOW not, O Athenians, how far you have been influenced by my accusers; for my part, in listening to them I almost forgot myself, so plausible were their arguments; however, so to speak, they have said nothing true. But of the many falsehoods which they have uttered I wondered at one of them especially, that in which they said you ought to be on your guard lest you should be deceived by me, as being eloquent in speech. For that they are not ashamed of being forthwith convicted by me in fact, when I shall show that I am not by any means eloquent, this seemed to me the most shameless thing in them, unless indeed they call him eloquent who speaks the truth.

[1] Delivered in Athens in 399 B.C., as reported by Plato in the "Apology." Translated by Henry Cary. Abridged.

For if they mean this, then I would allow that I am an orator, but not after their fashion; for they, as I affirm, have said nothing true; but from me you shall hear the whole truth. Not indeed, Athenians, arguments highly wrought, as theirs were, with choice phrases and expressions, nor adorned, but you shall hear a speech uttered without premeditation, in such words as first present themselves. For I am confident that what I say will be just, and let none of you expect otherwise; for surely it would not become my time of life to come before you like a youth with a got-up speech.

Above all things, therefore, I beg and implore this of you, O Athenians, if you hear me defending myself in the same language as that in which I am accustomed to speak both in the forum at the counters, where many of you have heard me, and elsewhere, not to be surprised or disturbed on this account. For the case is this: I now for the first time come before a court of justice, tho more than seventy years old; I am, therefore, utterly a stranger to the language here. As, then, if I were really a stranger, you would have pardoned me if I spoke in the language and the manner in which I had been educated, so now I ask this of you as an act of justice, as it appears to me, to disregard the manner of my speech, for perhaps it may be somewhat worse, and perhaps better, and to consider this only, and to give your attention to this, whether I speak what is just or not; for this is the virtue of a judge, but of an orator to speak the truth.

Perhaps, however, some one may say, "Are you not ashamed, Socrates, to have pursued a study from which you are now in danger of dying?" To such a person I should answer with good reason: You do not say well, friend, if you think that a man, who is even of the least value, ought to take into the account the risk of life or death, and ought not to consider that alone when he performs any action, whether he is acting justly or unjustly and the part of a good man or bad man.

I then should be acting strangely, O Athenians, if, when the generals whom you chose to command me assigned me my post at Potidæa, at Amphipolis, and at Delium, I then remained where they posted me, like any other person, and encountered the danger of death, but when the deity, as I thought and believed, assigned it as my duty to pass my life in the study of philosophy, and in examining myself and others, I should on that occasion, through fear of death or anything else whatsoever, desert my post. Strange indeed would it be, and then in truth any one might justly bring me to trial, and accuse me of not believing in the gods, from disobeying the oracle, fearing death, and thinking myself to be wise when I am not.

For to fear death, O Athenians, is nothing else than to appear to be wise without being so; for it is to appear to know what one does not know. For no one knows but that death is the greatest of all goods; but men feareth as if they well knew that it is the greatest of evils. And how is not this the most reprehensible ignorance, to think that one knows what one does not know?

But I, O Athenians, in this perhaps differ from most men; and if I should say that I am in anything wiser than another, it would be in this, that not having a competent knowledge of the things in Hades, I also think that I have not such knowledge. But to act unjustly, and to disobey my superior, whether God or man, I know is evil and base. I shall never, therefore, fear or shun things which, for aught I know, may be good, before evils which I know to be evils. So that even if you should now dismiss me, not yielding to the instances of Anytus, who said that either I should not appear here at all, or that, if I did appear, it was impossible not to put me to death, telling you that if I escaped, your sons, studying what Socrates teaches, would all be utterly corrupted; if you should address me thus, "Socrates, we shall not now yield to Anytus, but dismiss you, on this condition, however, that you no longer persevere in your researches nor study philosophy, and if hereafter you are detected in so doing, you shall die," —if, as I said, you should dismiss me on these terms, I should say to you:

"O Athenians, I honor and love you; but I shall obey God rather than you; and as long as I breathe and am able I shall not cease studying philosophy and exhorting you and warning any one of you I may happen to meet, saying, as I have been accustomed to do: 'O best of men, seeing you are an Athenian, of a city the most powerful and most renowned for wisdom and strength, are you not ashamed of being careful for riches, how you may acquire them in greatest abundance, and for glory and honor, but care not nor take any thought for wisdom and truth, and for your soul, how it may be made most perfect?' "

And if any one of you should question my assertion and affirm that he does care for these things, I shall not at once let him go, nor depart, but I shall question him, sift and prove him. And if he should appear to me not to possess virtue, but to pretend that he does, I shall reproach him for that he sets the least value on things of the greatest worth, but the highest on things that are worthless.

Murmur not, O Athenians, but continue to attend to my request, not to murmur at what I say, but to listen, for, as I think, you will derive benefit from listening. For I am going to say other things to you, at which perhaps you will raise a clamor; but on no account do so. Be well assured, then, if you put me to death, being such a man as I say I am, you will not injure me more than yourselves. For neither will Miletus nor Anytus harm me; nor have they the power; for I do not think that it is possible for a better man to be injured by a worse. He may perhaps have me condemned to death, or banished or deprived of civil rights, and he or others may perhaps consider these as mighty evils; I, however, do not consider them so, but that it is much more so to do what he is now doing—to endeavor to put a man to death unjustly.

Now, therefore, O Athenians, I am far from making a defense on my own behalf, as any one might think, but I do so on your behalf, lest by condemning me you should offend at all with respect to the gift of the deity to you. For, if you should put me to death, you will not easily find such another, tho it may be ridiculous to say so, altogether attached by the deity to this city as to a powerful and generous horse, somewhat sluggish from his size, and requiring to be roused by a gad-fly; so the deity appears to have united me, being such a person as I am, to the city, that I may rouse you, and persuade and reprove every one of you, nor ever cease besetting you throughout the whole day. Such another man, O Athenians, will not easily be found; therefore, if you will take my advice, you will spare me.

But you, perhaps, being irritated, like drowsy persons who are roused from sleep, will strike me, and, yielding to Anytus, will unthinkingly condemn me to death; and then you will pass the rest of your life in sleep, unless the deity, caring for you, should send some one else to you. But that I am a person who has been given by the deity to this city, you may discern from hence; for it is not like the ordinary conduct

of men that I should have neglected all my own
affairs and suffered my private interest to be
neglected for so many years, and that I should
constantly attend to your concerns, addressing
myself to each of you separately, like a father
or elder brother, persuading you to the pursuit
of virtue. And if I had derived any profit from
this course, and had received pay for my exhortations, there would have been some reason
for my conduct; but now you see yourselves that
my accusers, who have so shamelessly calumni-
ated me in everything else, have not had the
impudence to charge me with this, and to bring
witnesses to prove that I ever either exacted or
demanded any reward. And I think I produce
a sufficient proof that I speak the truth, namely,
my poverty.

Perhaps, however, it may appear absurd, that
I, going about, thus advise you in private and
make myself busy, but never venture to present
myself in public before your assemblies and give
advice to the city. The cause of this is that
which you have often and in many places heard
me mention: because I am moved by certain
divine and spiritual influence, which also Miletus, through mockery, has set out in the indictment. This began with me from childhood, being a kind of voice which, when present, always
diverts me from what I am about to do, but
never urges me on. This it is which opposed
my meddling in public politics; and it appears
to me to have opposed me very properly. For

be well assured, O Athenians, if I had long since attempted to intermeddle with politics, I should have perished long ago, and should not have at all benefited you or myself. And be not angry with me for speaking the truth. For it is not possible that any man should be safe, who sincerely opposes either you or any other multitude, and who prevents many unjust and illegal actions from being committed in a city; but it is necessary that he who in earnest contends for justice, if he will be safe for but a short time, should live privately, and take no part in public affairs.

Do you think, then, that I should have survived so many years if I had engaged in public affairs, and, acting as becomes a good man, had aided the cause of justice, and, as I ought, had deemed this of the highest importance? Far from it, O Athenians: nor would any other man have done so. But I, through the whole of my life, if I have done anything in public, shall be found to be a man, and the very same in private, who has never made a concession to any one contrary to justice, neither to any other, nor to any one of these whom my calumniators say are my disciples. I, however, was never the preceptor of any one; but if any one desired to hear me speaking and to see me busied about my own mission, whether he were young or old, I never refused him. Nor do I discourse when I receive money, and not when I do not receive any, but I allow both rich and poor alike to question me, and, if any one wishes it, to answer me and hear what I have to say. And for these, whether any one proves to be a good man or not, I cannot justly be responsible, because I never either promised them any instruction nor taught them at all. But if any one says that he has ever learned or heard anything from me in private, which all others have not, be well assured that he does not speak the truth.

But why do some delight to spend so long a time with me? Ye have heard, O Athenians. I have told you the whole truth that they delight to hear those closely questioned who think that they are wise but are not: for this is by no means disagreeable. But this duty, as I say, has been enjoined me by the deity, by oracles, by dreams, and by every mode by which any other divine decree has ever enjoined anything to man to do. These things, O Athenians, are both true, and easily confuted if not true. For if I am now corrupting some of the youths, and have already corrupted others, it were fitting, surely, that if any of them, having become advanced in life, had discovered that I gave them bad advice when they were young, they should now rise up against me, accuse me, and have me punished; or if they were themselves unwilling to do this, some of their kindred, their fathers, or brothers, or other relatives, if their kinsmen have ever sustained any damage from me, should now call it to mind.

Many of them, however, are here present,

whom I see. I could mention many to you, some one of whom certainly Miletus ought to have adduced in his speech as a witness. If, however, he then forgot to do so, let him now adduce them, I give him leave to do so, and let him say it, if he has anything of the kind to allege. But quite contrary to this, you will find, O Athenians, all ready to assist me, who have corrupted and injured their relatives, as Miletus and Anytus say. For those who have been themselves corrupted might perhaps have some reason for assisting me; but those who have not been corrupted, men now advanced in life, their relatives, what other reason can they have for assisting me, except that right and just one, that they know that Miletus speaks falsely and that I speak the truth.

Well then, Athenians; these are pretty much the things I have to say in my defense, and others perhaps of the same kind. Perhaps, however, some among you will be indignant on recollecting his own case, if he, when engaged in a cause far less than this, implored and besought the judges with many tears, bringing forward his children in order that he might excite their utmost compassion, and many others of his relatives and friends, whereas I do none of these things, altho I may appear to be incurring the extremity of danger. Perhaps, therefore, some one, taking notice of this, may become more determined against me, and, being enraged at this very conduct of mine, may give his vote under the influence of anger. If then any one of you is thus affected—I do not, however, suppose that there is—but if there should be, I think I may reasonably say to him: "I too, O best of men, have relatives; for to make use of that saying of Homer, I am not sprung from an oak, nor from a rock, but from men, so that I too, O Athenians, have relatives, and three sons, one now grown up, and two boys; I shall not, however, bring any one of them forward and implore you to acquit me." Why then shall I not do this?

Not from contumacy, O Athenians, nor disrespect toward you. Whether or not I am undaunted at the prospect of death, is another question, but out of regard to my own character, and yours, and that of the whole city, it does not appear to me to be honorable that I should do onything of this kind at my age, and with the reputation I have, whether true or false. For it is commonly agreed that Socrates in some respects excels the generality of men. If, then, those among you who appear to excel either in wisdom, or fortitude, or any other virtue whatsoever, should act in such a manner as I have often seen some when they have been brought to trial, it would be shameful, who, appearing indeed to be something, have conducted themselves in a surprising manner, as thinking they should suffer something dreadful by dying, and as if they would be immortal if you did put them to death. Such men appear to me to bring disgrace on the city, so that any stranger might suppose that such of the Athenians as excel in virtue, and whom they themselves choose in preference to themselves for magistracies and other honors, are in no respect superior to women.

For these things, O Athenians, neither ought we to do who have attained to any height of reputation, nor, should we do them, ought you to suffer us; but you should make this manifest, that you will much rather condemn him who introduces these piteous dramas, and makes the city ridiculous, than him who quietly awaits your decision.

But reputation apart, O Athenians, it does not appear to me to be right to entreat a judge, or to escape by entreaty, but one ought to inform and persuade him. For a judge does not sit for the purpose of administering justice out of favor, but that he may judge rightly, and he is sworn not to show favor to whom he pleases, but that he will decide according to the laws. It is therefore right that neither should we accustom you, nor should you accustom yourselves to violate your oaths; for in so doing neither of us would act righteously.

Think not then, O Athenians, that I ought to adopt such a course toward you as I neither consider honorable, nor just, nor holy, as well, by Jupiter, on any other occasion, and now especially when I am accused of impiety by this Miletus. For clearly, if I should persuade you, and by my entreaties should put a constraint on you who are bound by an oath, I should teach you to think that there are no gods, and in reality, while making my defense, should accuse myself of not believing in the gods. This, however, is far from being the case: for I believe, O Athenians, as none of my accusers do, and I leave it to you and to the deity to judge concerning me in such way as will be best both for me and for you.

II

ON BEING DECLARED GUILTY [1]
(399 B.C.)

THAT I should not be grieved, O Athenians, at what has happened, namely, that you have condemned me, as well as many other circumstances concur in bringing to pass, and moreover this, that what has happened has not happened contrary to my expectations; but I much rather wonder at the number of votes on either side. For I did not expect that I should be condemned by so small a number, but by a large majority; but now, as it seems, if only three more votes had changed sides I should have been acquitted. As far as Miletus is concerned, as it appears to

---

[1] After a majority of voices had declared him guilty, Socrates resumed his address as reported by Plato in the "Apology."

me, I have been already acquitted, and not only have I been acquitted, but it is clear to every one that had not Anytus and Lycon come forward to accuse me, he would have been fined a thousand drachmas, for not having obtained a fifth part of the votes.

The man then awards me the penalty of death. Well. But what shall I, on my part, O Athenians, award myself? Is it not clear that it will be such as I deserve? What then is that? Do I deserve to suffer or to pay a fine, for that I have purposely during my life not remained quiet, but, neglecting what most men seek after, —money-making, domestic concerns, military command, popular oratory, and moreover all the magistracies, conspiracies and cabals that are met with in the city,—thinking that I was in reality too upright a man to be safe if I took part in such things, I therefore did not apply myself to those pursuits, by attending to which I should have been of no service either to you or to myself; but in order to confer the greatest benefit on each of you privately, as I affirm, I thereupon applied myself to that object, endeavoring to persuade every one of you not to take any care of his own affairs, before he had taken care of himself, in what way he may become the best and wisest, nor of the affairs of the city before he took care of the city itself, and that he should attend to other things in the same manner.

What treatment then do I deserve, seeing I am such a man? Some reward, O Athenians, if at least I am to be estimated according to my real deserts; and moreover such a reward as would be suitable to me. What then is suitable to a poor man, a benefactor, and who has need of leisure in order to give you good advice? There is nothing so suitable, O Athenians, as that such a man should be maintained in the Prytaneum, and this much more than if one of you had been victorious at the Olympic games in a horse race, or in the two or four-horsed chariot race; for such a one makes you appear to be happy, but I, to be so: and he does not need support, but I do. If, therefore, I must award a sentence according to my just deserts, I award this, maintenance in the Prytaneum.

Perhaps, however, in speaking to you thus, I appear to you to speak in the same presumptuous manner as I did respecting commiseration and entreaties: but such is not the case, O Athenians, it is rather this. I am persuaded that I never designedly injured any man, tho I can not persuade you of this, for we have conversed with each other but for a short time. For if there was the same law with you as with other men, that in capital cases the trial should last not only one day but many, I think you would be persuaded; but it is not easy in a short time to do away with great calumnies.

Being persuaded then that I have injured no one, I am far from intending to injure myself, and of pronouncing against myself that I am deserving of punishment, and from awarding myself anything of the kind. Through fear of what? lest I should suffer that which Miletus awards me, of which I say I know not whether it be good or evil? instead of this, shall I choose what I well know to be evil, and award that? Shall I choose imprisonment? And why should I live in prison, a slave to the established magistracy, the Eleven? Shall I choose a fine, and to be imprisoned until I have paid it? But this is the same as that which I just now mentioned, for I have not money to pay it. Shall I then award myself exile? For perhaps you would consent to this award. I should indeed be very fond of life, O Athenians, if I were so devoid of reason as not to be able to reflect that you, who are my fellow citizens, have been unable to endure my manner of life and discourses, but they have become so burdensome and odious to you, that you now seek to be rid of them; others, however, will easily bear them; far from it, O Athenians. A fine life it would be for me at my age to go out wandering and driven from city to city, and so to live. For I well know that, wherever I may go, the youth will listen to me when I speak, as they do here. And if I repulse them they will themselves drive me out, persuading the elders; and if I do not repulse them, their fathers and kindred will banish me on their account.

Perhaps, however, some one will say, Can you not, Socrates, when you have gone from us, live a silent and quiet life? This is the most diffi-

cult thing of all to persuade some of you. For
if I say that that would be to disobey the deity,
and that therefore it is impossible for me to
live quietly, you would not believe me, thinking
I spoke ironically. If, on the other hand, I
say that this is the greatest good to man, to discourse daily on virtue, and other things which
you have heard me discussing, examining both
myself and others, but that a life without investigation is not worth living for, still less would
you believe me if I said this. Such, however, is
the case, as I affirm, O Athenians, tho it is not
easy to persuade you. And at the same time I
am not accustomed to think myself deserving of
any ill.

If, indeed I were rich, I would amerce myself
in such a sum as I should be able to pay; for
then I should have suffered no harm, but now—
for I can not, unless you are willing to amerce
me in such a sum as I am able to pay. But perhaps I could pay you a mina of silver; in that
sum then I amerce myself. But Plato here, O
Athenians, and Crito, Critobulus, and Apollo-
dorus bid me amerce myself in thirty minæ, and
they offer to be sureties. I amerce myself then
to you in that sum; and they will be sufficient
sureties for the money.

III

ON BEING CONDEMNED TO DEATH[1]

(399 B.C.)

FOR the sake of no long space of time, O Athenians, you will incur the character and reproach at the hands of those who wish to defame the city, of having put that wise man, Socrates, to death. For those who wish to defame you will assert that I am wise, tho I am not. If, then, you had waited for a short time, this would have happened of its own accord; for observe my age, that it is far advanced in life, and near death. But I say this not to you all, but to those only who have condemned me to die. And I say this too to the same persons. Perhaps you think, O Athenians, that I have been convicted through the want of arguments, by which I might have persuaded you, had I thought it right to do and say anything so that I might escape punishment. Far otherwise: I have been convicted through want indeed, yet not of arguments, but of audacity and impudence, and of the inclination to say such things to you as would have been most agreeable for you to hear, had I lamented and bewailed and done and said many other things unworthy of me, as I affirm, but such as you are accustomed to hear from others.

---

[1] When the judges had passed sentence condemning him to death, Socrates concluded his speech as here given.

But neither did I then think that I ought, for the sake of avoiding danger, to do anything unworthy of a freeman, nor do I now repent of having so defended myself; but I should much rather choose to die having so defended myself than to live in that way. For neither in a trial nor in battle is it right that I or any one else should employ every possible means whereby he may avoid death; for in battle it is frequently evident that a man might escape death by laying down his arms and throwing himself on the mercy of his pursuers. And there are many other devices in every danger, by which to avoid death, if a man dares to do and say everything.

But this is not difficult, O Athenians, to escape death, but it is much more difficult to avoid depravity, for it runs swifter than death. And now I, being slow and aged, am overtaken by the slower of the two; but my accusers, being strong and active, have been overtaken by the swifter, wickedness. And now I depart, condemned by you to death; but they condemned by truth, as guilty of iniquity and injustice: and I abide my sentence and so do they. These things, perhaps, ought so to be, and I think that they are for the best.

In the next place, I desire to predict to you who have condemned me, what will be your fate: for I am now in that condition in which men most frequently prophesy, namely, when they are about to die. I say then to you, O Athenians, who have condemned me to death, that immediately after my death a punishment will overtake you, far more severe, by Jupiter, than that which you have inflicted on me. For you have done this thinking you should be freed from the necessity of giving an account of your life. The very contrary however, as I affirm, will happen to you. Your accusers will be more numerous, whom I have now restrained, tho you did not perceive it; and they will be more severe, inasmuch as they are younger and you will be more indignant. For, if you think that by putting men to death you will restrain any one from upbraiding you because you do not live well, you are much mistaken; for this method of escape is neither possible nor honorable, but that other is most honorable and most easy, not to put a check upon others, but for a man to take heed to himself, how he may be most perfect. Having predicted thus much to those of you who have condemned me, I take my leave of you.

But with you who have voted for my acquittal, I would gladly hold converse on what has now taken place, while the magistrates are busy and I am not yet carried to the place where I must die. Stay with me then, so long, O Athenians, for nothing hinders our conversing with each other, whilst we are permitted to do so; for I wish to make known to you, as being my friends, the meaning of that which has just now befallen me. To me then, O my judges,—and in calling you judges I call you rightly,—a strange thing has happened. For the wonted prophetic voice

of my guardian deity, on every former occasion,
even in the most trifling affairs, opposed me, if
I was about to do anything wrong; but now, that
has befallen me which ye yourselves behold, and
which any one would think and which is supposed to be the extremity of evil, yet neither
when I departed from home in the morning did
the warning of the god oppose me, nor when I
came up here to the place of trial, nor in my
address when I was about to say anything; yet
on other occasions it has frequently restrained
me in the midst of speaking. But now it has never
throughout this proceeding opposed me, either
in what I did or said. What then do I suppose
to be the cause of this? I will tell you: what
has befallen me appears to be a blessing; and it
is impossible that we think rightly who suppose
that death is an evil. A great proof of this to
me is the fact that it is impossible but that the
accustomed signal should have opposed me, unless I had been about to meet with some good.

Moreover, we may hence conclude that there
is great hope that death is a blessing. For to
die is one of two things: for either the dead may
be annihilated and have no sensation of anything whatever; or, as it is said, there is a certain change and passage of the soul from one
place to another. And if it is a privation of all
sensation, as it were, a sleep in which the sleeper
has no dream, death would be a wonderful gain.
For I think that if anyone, having selected a
night in which he slept so soundly as not to have

had a dream, and having compared this night with all the other nights and days of his life, should be required on consideration to say how many days and nights he had passed better and more pleasantly than this night throughout his life, I think that not only a private person, but even a great king himself would find them easy to number in comparison with other days and nights. If, therefore, death is a thing of this kind, I say it is a gain; for thus all futurity appears to be nothing more than one night.

But if, on the other hand, death is a removal from hence to another place, and what is said be true, that all the dead are there, what greater blessing can there be than this, my judges? For if, on arriving at Hades, released from these who pretend to be judges, one shall find those who are true judges, and who are said to judge there, Minos and Rhadamanthus, Æacus and Triptolemus, and such others of the demigods as were just during their own life, would this be a sad removal? At what price would you not estimate a conference with Orpheus and Musæus, Hesiod and Homer? I indeed should be willing to die often, if this be true. For to me the sojourn there would be admirable, when I should meet with Palamedes, and Ajax son of Telamon, and any other of the ancients who has died by an unjust sentence. The comparing my sufferings with theirs would, I think, be no unpleasing occupation.

But the greatest pleasure would be to spend

my time in questioning and examining the people there as I have done those here, and discovering who among them is wise, and who fancies himself to be so but is not. At what price, my judges, would not any one estimate the opportunity of questioning him who led that mighty army against Troy, or Ulysses, or Sisyphus, or ten thousand others, whom one might mention, both men and women? with whom to converse and associate, and to question them, would be an inconceivable happiness. Surely for that the judges there do not condemn to death; for in other respects those who live there are more happy than those that are here, and are henceforth immortal, if at least what is said be true.

You, therefore, O my judges, ought to entertain good hopes with respect to death, and to meditate on this one truth, that to a good man nothing is evil, neither while living nor when dead, nor are his concerns neglected by the gods. And what has befallen me is not the effect of chance; but this is clear to me, that now to die, and be freed from my cares, is better for me. On this account the warning in no way turned me aside; and I bear no resentment toward those who condemned me, or against my accusers, altho they did not condemn and accuse me with this intention, but thinking to injure me: in this they deserve to be blamed.

Thus much, however, I beg of them. Punish my sons, when they grow up, O judges, paining them as I have pained you, if they appear to you to care for riches or anything else before virtue, and if they think themselves to be something when they are nothing, reproach them as I have done you, for not attending to what they ought, and for conceiving themselves to be something when they are worth nothing. If ye do this, both I and my sons shall have met with just treatment at your hands.

But it is now time to depart,—for me to die, for you to live. But which of us is going to a better state is unknown to every one but God.

ISOCRATES

ON THE UNION OF GREECE TO RESIST PERSIA [1]

(380 B.C.)

Born in 436 B.C., and died in 338; lived from the age of Pericles to that of Alexander; his teachings as to style influenced Plato, Demosthenes, and Cicero; usually classed as one of the ten Attic orators, but more properly a publicist.

IT is confessed indeed that our state is the most ancient and the greatest, and the most celebrated among all men; and the foundation being thus glorious, on account of what follows these it is still more befitting that we should be honored. For we inhabit this city, not having expelled others, nor having found it deserted, nor collected promiscuously from many nations, but we are of such honorable and genuine birth that we continue for all time possessing this land from which we were born, being sprung from the soil, and being able to call our city by the same names as our nearest relations, for we alone of all the Greeks have a right to call the same—nurse and fatherland and mother. And yet it is right that

[1] Supposed to have been first published at Olympia 380 B.C., and here abridged. It has been pointed out that, while the conquest of Asia by Alexander was not due to a union of Athens and Sparta, that achievement, in some other ways, was a justification of the plans advocated by Isocrates. Translated by Rev. James Rice. The writing and revising of this work are said to have been extended by Isocrates over a period of ten years.

those who with good reason entertain high
thoughts, and who justly dispute the supremacy
and who often make mention of their hereditary
rights, should prove the origin of their race to
be of this nature.

The advantages, then, which we possessed
from the beginning, and which were bestowed
upon us by fortune, are so great in magnitude;
but of how great advantages we have been the
cause to the rest we should thus best investigate,
if we should go through in detail the time from
the commencement, and the exploits of the State
in succession; for we shall find that she not only
[delivered us] from the dangers in respect of
war, but also is the cause of that established order
besides in which we dwell and with which we live
as free citizens, and by means of which we are
able to live.

Of the wars, indeed, the Persian was the most
famous; the old achievements, however, are not
less strong proofs for those who dispute about
hereditary institutions. For when Greece was
still in a lowly condition, the Thracians indeed
came to our land with Eumolpus the son of
Poseidon, and the Scythians with the Amazons
the daughters of Mars, not at the same time, but
at the time when each of them were rulers of
Europe, hating, indeed, the whole race of the
Greeks, but making charges against us separately, thinking that by this line of conduct they
would incur danger against one state indeed, but
would at the same time conquer all.

They did not, however, succeed, but having engaged with our ancestors separately, they were destroyed equally as if they had made war on all together. And the magnitude of the evils which befel them is manifest, for the speeches concerning them would never have lived on for so long a time had not also their achievements far excelled those of other men. It is recorded, then, concerning the Amazons, that not one of those who came went back again, while those who were left at home were driven out of their government on account of their calamity here; and concerning the Thracians, [it is said] that altho during the former times they dwelt beside us, on our borders, yet on account of that expedition they left so great an intervening space, that in the district between us, many nations and all kinds of races and great cities have been established.

Glorious indeed, then, are these things, and befitting those who dispute for the supremacy, but akin to what has been said, and such as it is natural that those sprung from such men would perform, were the exploits of those who waged war against Darius and Xerxes.

Always indeed, then, both our ancestors and the Lacedæmonians acted in a spirit of rivalry to each other. Not but what in those times they contended for the most glorious objects, not thinking each other to be enemies, but rivals, not paying court to the foreigner with a view to the slavery of the Greeks, but being of one mind about the common safety, and engaging in a contest as to this, viz., which of the two shall be the authors of it. And they displayed their valor first, indeed, in the case of those sent by Darius. For when these had landed in Attica, the one did not wait for their allies, but making what was a common war a personal one, they went out to meet those who had treated contemptuously the whole of Hellas with their private force, a few against many myriads, as if about to brave the danger in the case of the lives of others, while the others no sooner heard of the war being in Attica than, neglecting everything else they came to assist us, making as great haste as if it was their own country which was being ravaged.

And after these things, when the subsequent expedition took place, which Xerxes led in person, after abandoning his palace and undertaking to become a general, and having collected all the men from Asia; and who, being anxious not to speak in extravagant terms, has spoken about him in language which fell short of the reality? —a man, who reached such a height of arrogance, that considering it to be a trifling achievement to subdue Greece, and wishing to leave behind such a monument as surpasses human nature, ceased not until he had devised and at the same time carried out by compulsion that which all talk of, so that with his armament he sailed through the mainland and marched over the sea, having bridged over the Hellespont and dug a canal through Athos. Against him, indeed, having such high thoughts, and having succeeded in accomplishing such great deeds and having become the lord of so many, they went forth, having divided amongst themselves the danger, the Lacedæmonians indeed to Thermopylæ against the land force, having selected a thousand of themselves, and taking along with them a few of their allies with the intention of preventing them in the narrow pass from advancing farther, while our fathers [went out] to Artemisium, having manned sixty triremes to meet the whole naval force of the enemy. And they had the courage to do these things, not so much through contempt of the enemy as from a spirit of rivalry with each other, the Lacedæmonians indeed envying our state, for the battle at Marathon, and seeking to put themselves on an equality with us, and fearing lest our state should twice in succession become the author of deliverance to the Greeks, and our fathers wishing chiefly indeed to retain their present glory and to make it manifest to all that both in the former case it was through valor and not through fortune that they had conquered; in the next place also to induce the Greeks to maintain a sea-fight by showing to them that valor gets the better of numbers in naval dangers and enterprises equally as in those by land.

And to the king (of Asia), indeed, nothing is more important than to consider by what means we shall never cease warring against one another, while we are so far from bringing any of his interests into collision or causing them to be distracted by factions, that we even endeavor to assist in putting an end to the troubles which have befallen him through fortune; since we also allow him to make use of one of the two armaments in Cyprus, and to blockade the other, tho both of them belong to Hellas. For both those who have revolted are friendly disposed towards us and give themselves up to the Lacedæmonians, and the most useful part of those who are serving with Tiribazus and of the land army have been collected from these districts, and the greater part of the navy has sailed along with them from Ionia, who would much more gladly have ravaged Asia in concert than have fought against one another on account of trifles. Of these things we take no thought, but we are disputing about the islands of the Cyclades, and thus heedlessly have we surrendered to the foreign foe cities so many in number and so great in magnitude. Therefore, he is in possession of some, and is on the point of [taking possession of] others, and is plotting against others, having despised all of us, and with good reason. For he has effected what no one of his ancestors ever did; for it has been agreed on, both by us and by the Lacedæmonians, that Asia belongs to the king, and he has taken possession of the Grecian cities with such authority as to raze some of them to the ground, and in others to fortify citadels. And all these things have happened through our folly and not on account of his power.

Our citizens are at this time reconciled with
all the others with whom they have been at war,
and forget the hostility which has arisen, but to
the inhabitants of the continent they do not feel
grateful, even when they receive benefits [from
them], so undying is the anger they feel toward
them. And our fathers condemned many to
death for favoring the Medes; and even at the
present day, in their public assemblies, they
make imprecations, before they transact any
other business, on whomsoever of the citizens
makes proposals for peace to the Persians. And
the Eumolpidæ and the Heralds, in the celebra-
tion of the mysteries, on account of their hatred
for them, proclaim publicly also to all other foreigners, as they do to homicides, that they are
excluded from the sacred rites. And such hostile feelings do we entertain by nature toward
them, that even in our legends, we occupy ourselves with most pleasure with those relating to
the Trojan and Persian wars, by which it is possible to hear of their calamities. And one might
finds hymns composed in consequence of the war
against the foreigners, but dirges produced for
us in consequence of that against the Greeks, and
might find the former sung at the festivals,
while we call to mind the latter in our calamities. And I think that even the poetry of Homer
received greater honors, because he nobly extolled those who made war against the foreign
foe; and that for this reason our ancestors
wished to make his art honored, both in the con-

tests in poetry and in the education of the younger generation, in order that, hearing frequently his poems, we may learn by heart the enmity which existed toward them, and, emulating the deeds of valor of those who made war upon them, may set our hearts upon the same exploits as they achieved.

Wherefore there appear to me to be very many things which encourage us to make war against them, and especially the present favorable opportunity, than which nothing is more clear. And we must not let it slip. For, in fact, it is disgraceful not to use it when present, but to remember it when it is past. For what additional advantage could we even wish to have, if intending to go to war with the king, beyond what we already possess? Has not Egypt revolted from him, as well as Cyprus; and have not Phœnicia and Syria been devastated owing to the war; and has not Tyre, on account of which he was greatly elated, been seized by his enemies? And the majority of the cities in Cilicia those on our side possess, and the rest it is not difficult to acquire. But Lycia no one of the Persians ever conquered. And Hecatomnos, the overseer of Caria, in reality indeed has revolted for a long time already, and will confess it whenever we may wish. And from Cnidus to Sinope the Greeks inhabit the coasts of Asia, whom it is not necessary to persuade to go to war, but [only] not to prevent them.

And yet, as we already possess so many bases

of operation, and as so great a war encircles
Asia, what need is there too accurately to scrutinize what are likely to be the results? For where
they are inferior to small portions, it is not uncertain how they would be disposed, if they
should be compelled to war with all of us. Now
the case stands thus. If, indeed, the king occupy
in greater force the cities on the sea-coast, establishing in them greater garrisons than at present,
perhaps also those of the islands which are near
the mainland, as Rhodes and Samos and Chios,
might lean to his fortunes; but if we be the first
to seize them, it is probable that those inhabiting
Lydia and Phrygia, and the rest of the country
which lies above them, would be in the power of
those who make these their base of operations.
Wherefore it is necessary to hasten and to make
no loss of time, that we may not suffer what our
fathers did.

And it is fitting to make the expedition in the
present age, in order that those who participate
in the calamities may also have the enjoyment of
the advantages, and may not continue to live unfortunate during all their lifetime. For the time
past is sufficient—in which what horror is there
which has not happened?—for, tho there are
many evils already existing in the nature of man,
we ourselves have invented in addition more
than the necessary evils, having created wars and
factions among ourselves, so that some are
perishing lawlessly in their own cities, and some
are wandering in a foreign land with their chil-

dren and wives, and many being compelled, through want of the daily necessaries of life, to serve as mercenaries, are dying fighting against their friends on behalf of their enemies. And at this no one has ever ben indignant, but they think it becoming to shed tears at the calamities composed by poets, but, tho gazing upon many dreadful genuine sufferings happening on account of the war, they are so far from pitying them, that they even take more pleasure in the misfortunes of one another than in their own personal advantages. And perhaps, also, many might laugh at my simplicity, if I were to lament the misfortunes of individuals at such critical times, in which Italy has been devastated, and Sicily reduced to slavery, and so many cities have been surrendered to the foreigners, and the remaining portions of the Greeks are in the greatest dangers.

Now it is necessary to put out of the way these plottings, and to attempt those deeds from which we shall both inhabit our cities in greater security, and be more faithfully disposed to one another, and what is to be said about these matters is simple and easy. For it is neither possible to enjoy a secure peace, unless we make war in concert against the foreign enemy, nor for the Greeks to be of one mind until we consider both our advantages to come from one another, and our dangers to be against the same people.

But when these things have been done, and the embarrassment with regard to our means of living has been taken away, which both dissolves friendships and perverts relationships into enmity, and involves all men in wars and factions, it is not possible that we shall not be of one mind, and entertain toward one another genuine feelings of good will. For which reasons we must esteem it of the greatest importance how we shall, as soon as possible, banish the war from hence to the continent, as this is the only advantage we should reap from the dangers in fighting against one another, namely, if it should seem good to us to employ against the foreign foe the experience which we have derived from them.

And truly we shall not even annoy the cities by enrolling soldiers from them, a thing which is now most troublesome to them in the war against one another; for I think that those who will wish to stay at home will be much fewer in number than those who will desire to follow with us. For who, whether young or old, is so indifferent that he will not wish to have a share in this expedition, commanded indeed by the Athenians and Lacedæmonians, but collected in defense of the liberty of the allies, and sent out by the whole of Hellas, and marching to take vengeance upon the foreign foe? And how great must we consider the fame, and the memory, and the glory which those will either have in their lives, or leave behind them in their deaths, who have been the bravest in such exploits? For where those who made war against Alexander, and captured one city, were deemed worthy of such praises, what panegyrics must we expect that they will obtain who have conquered the whole of Asia? For who, either of those able to write poetry, or of those who understand how to speak, will not labor and study, wishing to leave behind him a memorial for all ages, at the same time of his own intellect and of their valor?

ISAEUS

IN THE SUIT AGAINST DICÆOGENES AND LEOCHARES [1]

Born about 420 B.C.; studied oratory under Isocrates, and became a teacher of Demosthenes; eleven of his speeches, relating chiefly to the law of inheritance, have survived.

You have heard the testimony of these witnesses, and I am persuaded that even Leochares himself will not venture to assert that they are perjured; but he will have recourse perhaps to his defense, that Dicæogenes has fully performed his agreement, and that his own office of surety is completely satisfied. If he allege this, he will speak untruly and will easily be confuted; for the clerk shall read to you a schedule of all the effects which Dicæogenes, the son of Menexenus, left behind him, together with an inventory of those which the defendant unjustly took; and if he affirms that our uncle neither had them in his lifetime nor left them to us at his death, let him prove his assertion; or if he insists that the goods were indeed ours, but that we had them restored to us, let him call a single witness to that fact; as we have produced evidence on our part that Dicæogenes promised to give us back the two-thirds of what the son of Menexenus possessed, and that Leochares undertook to see him

[1] Delivered in Athens. Translated by Sir William Jones. Abridged.

101

perform his promise. This is the ground of our action, and this we have sworn to be true. Let the oath again be read.

Now, judges, if the defendants intended only to clear themselves of this charge, what has already been said would be sufficient to ensure my success; but, since they are prepared to enter once more into the merits of the question concerning the inheritance, I am desirous to inform you on our side of all the transactions in our family; that, being apprised of the truth, and not deluded by their artifices, you may give a sentence agreeable to reason and justice.

Menexenus our grandfather had one son named Dicæogenes, and four daughters, of whom Polyaratus my father married one; another was taken by Democles of Phrearrhi; a third by Cephisophon of Pæania; and the fourth was espoused by Theopompus the father of Cephisodotus. Our uncle Dicæogenes, having sailed to Cnidos in the Parhalian galley, was slain in a sea fight; and, as he left no children, Proxenus the defendant's father brought a will to our parents, in which his son was adopted by the deceased and appointed heir to a third part of his fortune; this part our parents, unable at that time to contest the validity of the will, permitted him to take; and each of the daughters of Menexenus, as we shall prove by the testimony of persons then present, had a decree for her share of the residue.

When they had thus divided the inheritance

and had bound themselves by oath to acquiesce
in the division, each person possessed his allot-
ment for twelve years; in which time, tho the
courts were frequently open for the administration of justice, not one of these men thought of
alleging any unfairness in the transaction; un-
till, when the state was afflicted with troubles
and seditions, this Dicæogenes was persuaded by
Melas the Egyptian, to whom he used to submit
on other occasions, to demand from us all our
uncle's fortune and to assert that he was appointed heir to the whole.

When he began his litigation we thought he
was deprived of his senses; never imagining that
the same man, who at one time claimed as heir
to a third part, and at another time as heir to
the whole, could gain any credit before this tribunal; but when we came into court, altho we
urged more arguments than our adversary and
spoke with justice on our side, yet we lost our
cause; not through any fault of the jury, but
through the villainy of Melas and his associates,
who, taking advantage of the public disorders,
assumed a power of seizing possessions to which
they had no right, by swearing falsely for each
other. By such men, therefore, were the jury
deceived; and we, overcome by this abominable
iniquity, were stripped of our effects; for my
father died not long after the trial and before
he could prosecute, as he intended, the perjured
witnesses of his antagonist.

On the very day when Dicæogenes had thus

infamously prevailed against us, he ejected the
daughter of Cephisophon, the niece of him who
left the estate from the portion allotted to her;
took from the wife of Democles what her brother
had given her as coheiress; and deprived both
the mother of Cephisodotus and the unfortunate
youth himself of their whole fortune. Of all
these he was at the same time guardian and
spoiler, next of kin, and cruelest enemy; nor did
the relation which he bore them excite in the least
degree his compassion; but the unhappy orphans,
deserted and indigent, became destitute even of
daily necessities.

Such was the guardianship of Dicæogenes their
nearest kinsman! who gave to their avowed foes
what their father Theopompus had left them,
illegally possesses himself of the property which
they had from their maternal uncle and their
grandfather; and (what was the most open act
of cruelty) having purchased the house of their
father and demolished it, he dug up the ground
on which it stood, and made that handsome gar-
den for his own house in the city.

Still further, altho he receives an annual rent
of eighty minas from the estate of his uncle, yet
such are his insolence and profligacy that he sent
my cousin, Cephisodotus, to Corinth as a servile attendant on his brother Harmodius; and
adds to his other injuries this cruel reproach,
that he wears ragged clothes and coarse buskins;
but is not this unjust, since it was his own violence which reduced the boy to poverty?

On this point enough has been said. I now
return to the narration from which I have thus
disgressed. Menexenus then, the son of Cephisophon, and cousin both to this young man and to
me, having a claim to an equal portion of the
inheritance, began a prosecution against those
who had perjured themselves in the former
cause, and convicted Lycon, whom he had first
brought to justice, of having falsely sworn that
our uncle appointed this Dicæogenes heir to his
whole estate; when, therefore, this pretended
heir was disappointed in his hopes of deluding
you, he persuaded Menexenus, who was acting
both for our interest and his own, to make a
compromise, which, though I blush to tell it, his
baseness compels me to disclose.

What was their agreement?

That Menexenus should receive a competent
share of the effects on condition of his betraying
us, and of releasing the other false witnesses,
whom he had not yet convicted; thus, injured
by our enemies, and by our friends, we remained
with silent indignation.

Again, when contributions were continually
brought by all who loved their country, to support the war and provide for the safety of the
state, nothing came from Dicæogenes; when
Lechæum indeed was taken, and when he was
pressed by others to contribute, he promised publicly that he would give three minas, a sum less
than that which Cleonymus the Cretan voluntarily offered; yet even this promise he never

performed; but his name was hung up on the statues of the Eponymi with an inscription asserting, to his eternal dishonor, that he had not paid the contribution, which he promised in public, for his country's service. Who can now wonder, judges, that he deceived me, a private individual, when he so notoriously deluded you all in your common assembly? Of this transaction you shall now hear the proofs.

Such and so splendid have been the services which Dicæogenes, possessed of so large a fortune, has performed for the city. You perceive, too, in what manner he conducts himself toward his relations; some of whom he has deprived, as far as he was able, of their property; others he has basely neglected, and forced, through the want of mere necessaries to enter into the service of some foreign power. All Athens saw his mother sitting in the temple of Illithyia, and heard her accuse him of a crime which I blush to relate, but which he blushed not to commit. As to his friends, he has now incurred the violent hatred of Melas the Egyptian, who had been fond of him in his early youth, by refusing to pay him a sum of money which he had borrowed; his other companions he had either defrauded of sums which they lent him, or has failed to perform his promise of giving them part of his plunder if he succeeded in his cause.

Yet our ancestors, judges, who first acquired this estate, and left it to their descendants, conducted all the public games, contributed liberally toward the expense of the war, and continually had the command of galleys, which they equipped: of these noble acts the presents with which they were able, from what remained of their fortune after their necessary charges, to decorate the temples, are no less undeniable proofs, than they are lasting monuments of their virtue; for they dedicated to Bacchus the tripods which they won by their magnificence in their games; they gave new ornaments to the temple of the Pythian Apollo, and adorned the shrine of the goddess in the citadel, where they offered the first fruits of their estate, with a great number, if we consider that they were only private men, of statues both in brass and stone, they died fighting resolutely in defence of their country; for Dicæogenes, the father of my grandfather, Menexenus, fell at the head of the Olysian legion in Spartolus; and his son, my uncle, lost his life at Cnidos, where he commanded the Parhaliar galley.

His estate, O Dicæogenes, thou hast unjustly seized and shamefully wasted, and, having converted it into money, hast the assurance to complain of poverty. How hast thou spent that money? Not for the use of the state or of your friends; since it is apparent that no part of it has been employed for those purposes; not in breeding fine horses, for thou never wast in possession of a horse worth more than three minas; not in chariots, for, with so many farms and so great a fortune, thou never hadst a single carriage even drawn by mules; nor hast thou redeemed any citizen from captivity; nor hast thou conveyed to the citadel those statues which Menexenus had ordered to be made for the price of three talents, but was prevented by his death from consecrating in the temple; and, through thy avarice, they lie to this day in the shop of the statuary; thus hast thou presumed to claim an estate to which thou hast no color of right, and hast not restored to the gods the statues, which were truly their own.

On what ground, Dicæogenes, canst thou ask the jury to give a sentence in thy favor? Is it because thou hast frequently served the public offices; expended large sums of money to make the city more respectable, and greatly benefited the state by contributing bountifully toward supporting the war? Nothing of this sort can be alleged with truth. Is it because thou art a valiant soldier? But thou never once could be persuaded to serve in so violent and formidable a war, in which even the Olynthians and the islanders lose their lives with eagerness, since they fight for this country; whilst thou, who art a citizen, wouldst never take arms for the city.

Perhaps the dignity of thy ancestors, who slew the tyrant, emboldens thee to triumph over us: as for them, indeed, I honor and applaud them, but cannot think that a spark of their virtue animates thy bosom; for thou hast preferred the plunder of our inheritance to the glory of being their descendant, and wouldst rather be called the son of Dicæogenes than of Harmodius; not regarding the right of being entertained in the Prytaneum, nor setting any value on the precedence and immunities which the posterity of those heroes enjoy: yet it was not for noble birth that Harmonius and Aristogiton were so transcendently honored, but for their valor and probity; of which thou, Dicæogenes, hast not the smallest share.

DEMOSTHENES

I

THE SECOND ORATION AGAINST PHILIP [1]
(344 B.C.)

Born in 384 B.C., died in 322; entered public life when about twenty-five years old, "and from that time till his death his history is the history of Athens"; sixty of his speeches preserved, tho some probably are spurious; his masterpiece, indeed the masterpiece of oratory, is "The Oration on the Crown."

ATHENIANS! when the hostile attempts of Philip, and those outrageous violations of the peace which he is perpetually committing, are at any time the subject of our debates, the speeches on your side I find humane and just, and that the sentiments of those who inveigh against Philip never fail of approbation; but as to the necessary measures, to speak out plainly, not one has been pursued, nor anything effected even to reward the attention to these harangues. Nay, to such circumstances is our state reduced, that the more fully and evidently a man proves that Philip is acting contrary to his treaty, and harboring designs against Greece, the greater is his difficulty in pointing out your duty.

The reason is this. They who aspire to an extravagant degree of power are to be opposed

[1] Delivered in Athens about 344 B.C. Translated by Thomas Leland. Abridged.

by force and action, not by speeches; and yet in the first place, we public speakers are unwilling to recommend or to propose anything to this purpose, from the fear of your displeasure; but confine ourselves to general representations of the grievous, of the outrageous nature of his conduct, and the like. Then you who attend are better qualified than Philip, either to plead the justice of your cause or to apprehend it when enforced by others; but as to any effectual opposition to his present designs, in this you are entirely inactive. You see, then, the consequence, the necessary, the natural consequence, each of you excels in that which has engaged your time and application, he in acting, you in speaking. And if, on this occasion, it be sufficient that we speak with a superior force of truth and justice, this may be done with the utmost ease; but if we are to consider how to rectify our present disorders, how to guard against the danger of plunging inadvertently into still greater, against the progress of a power which may at last bear down all opposition—then must our debates proceed in a different manner; and all they who speak, and all you who attend, must prefer the best and most salutary measures to the easiest and most agreeable.

First, then, Athenians, if there be a man who feels no apprehensions at the view of Philip's power, and the extent of his conquests, who imagines that these portend no danger to the state, or that his designs are not all aimed against you, I am amazed! and must entreat the attention of you all while I explain those reasons briefly which induce me to entertain different expectations, and to regard Philip as our real enemy; that if I appear to have looked forward with the more penetrating eye, you may join with me; if they who are thus secure and confident in this man, you may yield to their direction.

In the first place, therefore, I consider the acquisitions made by Philip, when the peace was just concluded, Thermopylæ, and the command of Phocis. What use did he make of these? He chose to serve the interest of Thebes, not that of Athens. And why? As ambition is his great passion, universal empire the sole object of his views; not peace, not tranquillity, not any just purpose: he knew this well, that neither our constitution nor our principles would admit him to prevail on you by anything he could promise, by anything he could do, to sacrifice one state of Greece to your private interest; but that, as you have the due regard to justice, as you have an abhorrence of the least stain on your honor, and as you have that quick discernment which nothing can escape, the moment his attempt was made, you would oppose him with the same vigor as if you yourselves had been immediately attacked. The Thebans, he supposed (and the event confirmed his opinion), would, for the sake of any private advantage, suffer him to act toward others as he pleased; and far from opposing or impeding his designs, would be ready at his command to fight on his side. From the same persuasion he now heaps his favors on the Messenians and Argians. And this reflects the greatest luster on you, my countrymen; for by these proceedings you are declared the only invariable assertors of the rights of Greece—the only persons, whom no private attachment, no views of interest, can seduce from their affection to the Greeks.

And that it is with reason he entertains these sentiments of you, and sentiments so different of the Thebans and the Argians, he may be convinced, not from the present only, but from a review of former times; for he must have been informed, I presume he cannot but have heard, that your ancestors, when, by submitting to the king, they might have purchased the sovereignty of Greece, not only scorned to listen when Alexander, this man's ancestor, was made the messenger of such terms, but chose to abandon their city, encountered every possible difficulty, and after all this performed such exploits as men are ever eager to recite, yet with the just force and dignity no man could ever express; and therefore it becomes me to be silent on this subject; for in reality their actions are superior to the power of words. As to the ancestors of the Thebans and the Argians, the one, he knows, fought for the barbarian; the others did not oppose him. He knew, then, that both these people would attend but their private interest, without the least regard to the common cause of Greece. Should he choose you for allies, you would serve him so far only as justice would permit; but if he attached himself to them, he gained assistants in all the schemes of his ambition. This it is that then determined him, this it is that now determines him to their side rather than to yours: not that he sees they have a greater naval force than we; or that, having gained the sovereignty in the inland countries, he declines the command of the seas and the advantages of commerce; or that he has forgotten those pretenses, those promises which obtained him the peace.

But I may be told: It is true, he did act thus; but not from ambition, or from any of those motives of which I accuse him; but as he thought the cause of Thebes more just than ours. This of all pretenses he cannot now allege. Can he, who commands the Lacedæmonians to quit their claim to Messene, pretend that, in giving up Orchomenus and Coronea to the Thebans, he acted from regard to justice? But now comes his last subterfuge. He was compelled, and yielded these places quite against his inclinations, being encompassed by the Thessalian horse and Theban infantry. Fine pretense! Just so, they cry, he is to entertain suspicions of the Thebans; and some spread rumors of their own framing, that he is to fortify Elatea. Yes! these things are yet to be, and so will they remain, in my

opinion; but his attack on Lacedæmon, in conjunction with the Thebans and Argians, is not
yet to be made. No: he is actually detaching
forces, supplying money, and is himself expected at the head of a formidable army. The Lacedæmonians, therefore, the enemies of Thebes, he
now infests. And will he then restore the
Phocians, whom he has but just now ruined?
Who can believe this? I, for my part, can never
think, if Philip had been forced into those former
measures, or if he had now abandoned the Thebans, that he would make this continued opposition to their enemies. No, his present measures
prove that all his past conduct was the effect
of choice; and from all his actions, it appears
that all his actions are directly leveled against
this state; and there is in some sort a necessity
for this. Consider, he aims at empire, and from
you alone he expects opposition. He has long
loaded us with injuries; and of this he himself
is most intimately conscious; for those of our
possessions which he has reduced to his service
he uses as a barrier to his other territories: so
that, if he should give up Amphipolis and Potidæa, he would not think himself secure even in
Macedon. He is therefore sensible that he entertains designs against you, and that you perceive
them. Then, as he thinks highly of your wisdom, he concludes that you must hold him in
that abhorrence which he merits; hence is he
alarmed, expecting to feel some effects of your
resentment (if you have any favorable oppor-

tunity) unless he prevent you by his attack.
Hence is his vigilance awakened; his arm raised
against the state; he courts some of the Thebans,
and such of the Peloponnesians as have the same
views with him; whom he deems too mercenary
to regard anything but present interest, and
too perversely stupid to foresee any consequences. And yet persons of but moderate discernment may have some manifest examples to alarm
them, which I had occasion to mention to the
Messenians and to the Argians. Perhaps it may
be proper to repeat them here.

"Messenians!" said I, "how highly, think
ye, would the Olynthians have been offended if
any man had spoken against Philip at that time
when he gave them up Anthemus, a city which
the former kings of Macedon had ever claimed?
when he drove out the Athenian colony, and gave
them Potidæa? when he took all our resentment on himself, and left them to enjoy our
dominions? Did they expect to have suffered
thus? Had it been foretold, would they have believed it? You cannot think it! Yet, after a
short enjoyment of the territories of others,
they have been forever despoiled of their own
by this man. Inglorious has been their fall,
not conquered only, but betrayed and sold by
one another; for those intimate correspondences
with tyrants ever portend mischief to free
states."—"Turn your eyes," said I, "to the
Thessalians! think ye, that when he first expelled their tyrants, when he then gave them up

Nicæa and Magnesia, that they expected ever
to have been subjected to those governors now
imposed on them? or that the man who restored
them to their seat in the amphictyonic council
would have deprived them of their own proper
revenues? yet, that such was the event, the world
can testify. In like manner, you now behold
Philip lavishing his gifts and promises on you.
If you are wise, you will pray that he may
never appear to have deceived and abused you.
Various are the contrivances for the defense and
security of cities; as battlements, and walls, and
trenches, and every other kind of fortification;
all which are the effects of labor, and attended
with continual expense. But there is one common bulwark with which men of prudence are
naturally provided, the guard and security of
all people, particularly of free states, against the
assaults of tyrants. What is this? Distrust. Of
this be mindful: to this adhere: preserve this
carefully, and no calamity can affect you."—
"What is it you seek?" said I. "Liberty? And
do ye not perceive that nothing can be more
adverse to this than the very titles of Philip?
Every monarch, every tyrant is an enemy to
liberty, and the opposer of laws. Will ye not
then be careful lest, while ye seek to be freed
from war, you find yourselves his slaves?"

It would be just, Athenians, to call the men
before you who gave those promises which induced you to conclude the peace; for neither
would I have undertaken the embassy, nor would

you, I am convinced, have laid down your arms, had it been suspected that Philip would have acted thus when he had obtained peace. No: the assurances he then gave were quite different from the present actions. There are others also to be summoned. Who are these? The men who, at my return from the second embassy (sent for the ratification of the treaty[1]), when I saw the state abused, and warned you of your danger, and testified the truth, and opposed with all my power the giving up Thermopylæ and Phocis— the men, I say, who then cried out that I, the water-drinker, was morose and peevish; but that Philip, if permitted to pass, would act agreeably to your desires; would fortify Thespia and Platæa; restrain the insolence of Thebes; cut through the Chersonesus at his own expense, and give you up Eubœa and Oropus, as an equivalent for Amphipolis. That all this was positively affirmed you cannot, I am sure, forget, tho not remarkable for remembering injuries. And, to complete the disgrace, you have engaged your posterity to the same treaty, in full dependence on those promises; so entirely have you been seduced.

And now, to what purpose do I mention this? and why do I desire that these men should appear? I call the gods to witness, that without

---

[1] The Peace of 343 B.C. is here referred to. It lasted for six years. During this period Philip was constantly engaged in those intrigues against Athens which became the subjects of the Second and Third Philippics and other orations by Demosthenes.

the least evasion I shall boldly declare the truth! Not that, by breaking out into invectives, I may expose myself to the like treatment, and once more give my old enemies an opportunity of receiving Philip's gold; nor yet that I may indulge an impertinent vanity of haranguing; but I apprehend the time must come when Philip's actions will give you more concern than at present. His designs, I see, are ripening. I wish my apprehensions may not prove just; but I fear that time is not far off. And when it will no longer be in your power to disregard events; when neither mine nor any other person's information, but your own knowledge, your own senses will assure you of the impending danger, then will your severest resentment break forth. And as your ambassadors have concealed certain things, influenced (as they themselves are conscious) by corruption, I fear that they who endeavor to restore what these men have ruined may feel the weight of your displeasure; for there are some, I find, who generally point their anger, not at the deserving objects, but those most immediately at their mercy.

While our affairs, therefore, remain not absolutely desperate—while it is yet in our power to debate—give me leave to remind you all of one thing, tho none can be ignorant of it. Who was the man that persuaded you to give up Phocis and Thermopylæ? which once gained, he also gained free access for his troops to Attica and to Peloponnesus, and obliged us to turn our thoughts from the rights of Greece, from all foreign interests, to a defensive war, in these very territories; whose approach must be severely felt by every one of us; and that very day gave birth to it; for had we not been then deceived, the state could have nothing to apprehend. His naval power could not have been great enough to attempt Attica by sea; nor could he have passed by land through Thermopylæ and Phocis. But he must have either confined himself within the bounds of justice and lived in a due observance of his treaty, or have instantly been involved in a war equal to that which obliged him to sue for peace.

Thus much may be sufficient to recall past actions to your view. May all the gods forbid that the event should confirm my suspicions! for I by no means desire that any man should meet even the deserved punishment of his crimes, when the whole community is in danger of being involved in his destruction.

II

ON THE STATE OF THE CHERSONESUS[1]
(342 B.C.)

IT were to be wished, Athenians, that they who speak in public would never suffer hatred or affection to influence their counsels; but, in

---

[1] Delivered in Athens about 342 B.C., or two years later than the Second Philippic. Translated by Thomas Leland.

Chersonesus is the Greek word for a peninsula. In this oration

all that they propose, be directed by unbiased reason; particularly when affairs of state, and those of highest moment, are the object of our attention. But since there are persons whose speeches are partly dictated by a spirit of contention, partly by other like motives, it is your duty, Athenians, to exert that power which your numbers give you, and in all your resolutions and in all your actions to consider only the interest of your country.

Our present concernment is about the affairs of the Chersonesus, and Philip's expedition into Thrace, which has now engaged him eleven months; but most of our orators insist on the actions and designs of Diopithes. As to crimes objected to those men whom our laws can punish when we please, I, for my part, think it quite indifferent whether they be considered now or at some other time; nor is this a point to be violently contested by me or any other speaker. But when Philip, the enemy of our country, is now actually hovering about the Hellespont[1] with a numerous army, and making attempts on our dominions, which, if one moment neglected, the loss may be irreparable; here our attention is instantly demanded; we should re-

Chersonesus Thracica is referred to, the same being the modern peninsula of Gallipoli, lying between the Hellespont and the Gulf of Melas.

[1] By the Hellespont Mr. Leland explains, in one of his notes, that we are here to understand not the strait itself that separates Europe from Asia, but the cities and countries along the coast line.

solve, we should prepare with all possible expedition, and not run from our main concern in the midst of foreign clamors and accusations.

I have frequently been surprised at assertions made in public; but never more than when I lately heard it affirmed in the senate, that there are but two expedients to be proposed—either absolutely to declare war, or to continue in peace. The point is this: if Philip acts as one in amity with us; if he does not keep possession of our dominions contrary to his treaty; if he be not everywhere spiriting up enemies against us, all debates are at an end; we are undoubtedly obliged to live in peace, and I find it perfectly agreeable to you. But if the articles of our treaty, ratified by the most solemn oaths, remain on record, open to public inspection; if it appears that long before the departure of Diopithes and his colony, who are now accused of involving us in a war, Philip had unjustly seized many of our possessions (for which I appeal to your own decrees); if, ever since that time, he has been constantly arming himself with all the powers of Greeks and Barbarians to destroy us—what do these men mean who affirm we are either absolutely to declare war, or to observe the peace? You have no choice at all; you have but one just and necessary measure to pursue, which they industriously pass over. And what is this? To repel force by force. Unless they will affirm, that while Philip keeps from Attica and the Piræus, he does our state no injury, makes no war against us. If it be thus they state the bounds of peace and justice, we must all acknowledge that their sentiments are inconsistent with the common rights of mankind—with the dignity and the safety of Athens.

Besides, they themselves contradict their own accusation of Diopithes. For shall Philip be left at full liberty to pursue all his other designs, provided he keeps from Attica; and shall not Diopithes be permitted to assist the Thracians? And if he does, shall we accuse him of involving us in a war? But this is their incessant cry: "Our foreign troops commit outrageous devastations on the Hellespont: Diopithes, without regard to justice, seizes and plunders vessels! These things must not be suffered." Be it so; I acquiesce! but while they are laboring to have our troops disbanded, by inveighing against that man whose care and industry support them (if they really speak from a regard to justice), they should show us, that if we yield to their remonstrances Philip's army also will be disbanded: but it is apparent that their whole aim is to reduce the state to those circumstances which have occasioned all the losses we have lately suffered. For, be assured of this, that nothing has given Philip such advantage over us as his superior vigilance in improving all opportunities. For, as he is constantly surrounded by his troops, and his mind perpetually engaged in projecting his designs, he can in a moment strike the blow where he pleases. But we wait till some event alarms us; then we are in motion; then we prepare. To this alone I can impute it, that the conquests he has lately made he now enjoys in full security; while all your efforts are too late, all your vast expenses ineffectual; your attempts have served only to discover your enmity and inclination to oppose him; and the consequences of your misconduct are still further aggravated by the disgrace.

Know, then, Athenians, that all our orators allege at present are but words, but idle pretenses. Their whole designs, their whole endeavors are to confine you within the city; that while we have no forces in the field, Philip may be at full liberty to act as he pleases. Consider the present posture of affairs. Philip is now stationed in Thrace, at the head of a large army, and (as we are here informed) sends for reinforcements from Macedon and Thessaly. Now, should he watch the blowing of the Etesian winds, march his forces to Byzantium, and invest it; in the first place, can you imagine that the Byzantines would persist in their present folly; or that they would not have recourse to you for assistance? I cannot think it. No: if there were people in whom they less confided than in us, they would receive even these into their city rather than give it up to him, unless prevented by the quickness of his attack. And should we be unable to sail thither, should there be no forces ready to support them, nothing can prevent their ruin. "But the ex-

travagance and folly of these men exceed all
bounds." I grant it. Yet still they should be
secured from danger; for this is the interest of
our state. Besides, it is by no means clear that
he will not march into the Chersonesus itself.
On the contrary, if we may judge from the letter
which he sent to you, he is determined to oppose us in that country. If then the forces
stationed there be still kept up, we may defend
our own dominions, and infest those of our
enemy; if they be once dispersed and broken,
what shall we do if he attempt the Chersonesus?
"Bring Diopithes to a trial." And how will
that serve us? "No: but we will dispatch succors from hence." What if the winds prevent
us? "But he will not turn his arms thither."
Who will be our surety for this? Consider, Athenians, is not the season of the year approaching
in which it is thought by some that you are
to withdraw your forces from the Hellespont,
and abandon it to Philip? But suppose (for
this too merits our attention) that at his return
from Thrace he should neither bend his force
against the Chersonesus nor Byzantium, but fall
on Chalcis or Megara, as he lately did on
Oreum; which would be the wiser course, to
oppose him here, and make Attica the seat of
war, or to find him employment abroad? I think
the latter.

Let these things sink deep into our minds;
and let us not raise invidious clamors against
those forces which Diopithes is endeavoring to

keep up for the service of his country, or attempt to break them: let us rather prepare to reinforce them; grant their general the necessary supplies of money, and in every other instance favor his designs with a hearty zeal. Imagine this question proposed to Philip: "Which would be most agreeable to you, that the forces commanded by Diopithes"—of whatever kind they be, for I shall not dispute on that head—"should continue in full strength and good esteem at Athens, and be reinforced by detachments from the city; or that the clamors and invectives of certain persons should prevail to have them broken and disbanded?" I think he would choose this latter. And are there men among us laboring for that which Philip would entreat the gods to grant him? And if so, is it still a question whence our distresses have arisen?

Let me entreat you to examine the present state of Athens with an unbiased freedom; to consider how we are acting, and how our affairs are conducted. We are neither willing to raise contributions, nor do we dare to take the field, nor do we spare the public funds, nor do we grant supplies to Diopithes, nor do we approve of those subsidies he has procured himself; but we malign him, we pry into his designs, and watch his motions. Thus we proceed, quite regardless of our interests; and while in words we extol those speakers who assert the dignity of their country, our actions favor their opposers.

It is usual, when a speaker rises to ask him, "What are we to do?" Give me leave to propose the like question to you: "What am I to say?" For, if you neither raise contributions, nor take the field, nor spare the public funds, nor grant subsidies to Diopithes, nor approve of those provisions he has made himself, nor take the due care of our interests, I have nothing to say. If you grant such unbounded license to informers as even to listen to their accusations of a man for what they pretend he will do, before it be yet done, what can one say?

But it is necessary to explain to some of you the effect of this behavior. (I shall speak with an undaunted freedom, for in no other manner can I speak.) It has been the constant custom of all the commanders who have sailed from this city (if I advance a falsehood let me feel the severest punishment) to take money from the Chians, and from the Erythrians, and from any people that would give it; I mean of the inhabitants of Asia. They who have but one or two ships take a talent; they who command a greater force raise a larger contribution; and the people who give this money, whether more or less, do not give it for nothing (they are not so mad); no, it is the price they pay to secure their trading vessels from rapine and piracy, to provide them with the necessary convoys, and the like, however, they may pretend friendship and affection, and dignify those payments with the name of free gifts. It is therefore evident, that as Diopithes is at the head of a considerable power, the same contributions will be granted to him. Else how shall he pay his soldiers? how shall he maintain them, who receives nothing from you, and has nothing of his own? From the skies? No; but from what he can collect, and beg, and borrow. So that the whole scheme of his accusers is to warn all people to grant him nothing, as he is to suffer punishment for crimes yet to be committed, not for any he has already committed, or in which he has already assisted. This is the meaning of their clamors. "He is going to form sieges! he leaves the Greeks exposed." Have these men all this tenderness for the Grecian colonies of Asia? They then prefer the interests of foreigners to that of their own country. This must be the case, if they prevail to have another general sent to the Hellespont. If Diopithes commits outrages—if he be guilty of piracy, one single edict, Athenians— a single edict will put a stop to such proceedings. This is the voice of our laws; that such offenders should be impeached, and not opposed with such vast preparations of ships and money (this would be the height of madness): it is against our enemies, whom the laws cannot touch, that we ought, we must maintain our forces, send out our navies, and raise our contributions. But when citizens have offended, we can decree, we can impeach, we can recall. These are arms sufficient; these are the measures befitting men of prudence: they who would raise disorder and

confusion in the state may have recourse to such
as these men propose.

But dreadful as it is to have such men among
us, yet the most dreadful circumstance of all is
this. You assemble here, with minds so disposed, that if any one accuses Diopithes, or
Chares, or Aristophon, or any citizen whatever,
as the cause of our misfortunes, you instantly
break forth into acclamations and applause. But
if a man stands forth, and thus declares the
truth: "This is all trifling, Athenians! It is
to Philip we owe our calamities: he has plunged
us in these difficulties; for had he observed his
treaty, our state would be in perfect tranquillity!" This you cannot deny; but you hear it
with the utmost grief, as if it were the account
of some dreadful misfortune. The cause is this
(for when I am to urge the interest of my
country, let me speak boldly): certain persons
who have been intrusted with public affairs have
for a long time past rendered you daring and
terrible in council, but in all affairs of war
wretched and contemptible. Hence it is, that
if a citizen, subject to your own power and
jurisdiction, be pointed out as the author of
your misfortunes, you hear the accusation with
applause; but if they are charged on a man who
must first be conquered before he can be punished, then you are utterly disconcerted; that truth
is too severe to be borne. Your ministers, Athenians, should take a quite contrary course. They
should render you gentle and humane in coun-

cil, where the rights of citizens and allies come before you; in military affairs they should inspire you with fierceness and intrepidity; for here you are engaged with enemies, with armed troops. But now, by leading you gently on to their purposes, by the most abject compliance with your humors, they have so formed and molded you that in your assemblies you are delicate, and attend but to flattery and entertainment, in your affairs you find yourselves threatened with extremity of danger.

And now, in the name of Heaven! suppose that the states of Greece should thus demand an account of those opportunities which your indolence has lost: "Men of Athens! you are ever sending embassies to us; you assure us that Philip is projecting our ruin, and that, of all the Greeks, you warn us to guard against this man's designs." (And it is too true we have done thus.) "But, O most wretched of mankind! when this man has been ten months detained abroad; when sickness, and the severity of winter, and the armies of his enemies rendered it impossible for him to return home, you neither restored the liberty of Eubœa nor recovered any of your own dominions. But while you sit at home in perfect ease and health (if such a state may be called health), Eubœa is commanded by his two tyrants; the one, just opposite to Attica, to keep you perpetually in awe; the other to Scyathus. Yet you have not attempted to oppose even this. No; you have submitted; you

have been insensible to your wrongs; you have
fully declared that if Philip were ten times to
die, it would not inspire you with the least
degree of vigor. Why, then, these embassies,
these accusations, all this unnecessary trouble to
us?'' If they should say this, what could we
allege? what answer could we give? I know not.

We have those among us who think a speaker
fully confuted by asking, ''What, then, is to be
done?'' To whom I answer, with the utmost
truth and justness, ''Not what we are now
doing.'' But I shall be more explicit if they will
be as ready to follow as to ask advice.

First then, Athenians, be firmly convinced of
these truths: that Philip does commit hostilities
against us, and has violated the peace (and let
us no longer accuse each other of his crimes);
that he is the implacable enemy of this whole
city, of the ground on which this city stands,
of every inhabitant within these walls, even of
those who imagine themselves highest in his
favor. If they doubt this, let them think of
Euthycrates and Lasthenes, the Olynthians. They
who seemed the nearest to his heart, the moment
they betrayed their country were distinguished
only by the superior cruelty of their death.
But it is against our constitution that his arms
are principally directed; nor, in all his schemes,
in all his actions, has he anything so immediately in view as to subvert it. And there is some
sort of a necessity for this. He knows full well
that his conquests, however great and extensive,

can never be secure while you continue free;
but that, if once he meets with any accident
(and every man is subject to many), all those
whom he has forced into his service will instantly
revolt, and fly to you for protection; for you are
not naturally disposed to grasp at empire yourselves, but to frustrate the ambitious attempts of
others; to be ever ready to oppose usurpation,
and assert the liberty of mankind; this is your
peculiar character. And therefore it is not
without regret that he sees in your freedom a
spy on the incidents of his fortune. Nor is this
his reasoning weak or trivial.

In the first place, therefore, we are to consider him as the enemy of our state, the implacable enemy of our free constitution. Nothing
but the deepest sense of this can give you a
true, vigorous, and active spirit. In the next
place, be assured that everything he is now
laboring, everything he is concerting, he is concerting against our city; and that wherever any
man opposes him, he opposes an attempt against
these walls; for none of you can be weak enough
to imagine that Philip's desires are centered in
those paltry villages of Thrace (for what name
else can one give to Drongilus, and Cabyle, and
Mastira, and all those places he is now reducing
to his obedience?); that he endures the severity
of toils and seasons, and braves the utmost dangers for these, and has no designs on the ports,
and the arsenals, and the navies, and the silver
mines, and all the other revenues of Athens,

but that he will leave them for you to enjoy; while for some wretched hoards of grain in the cells of Thrace he takes up his winter quarters in the horrors of a dungeon. Impossible! No; these and all his expeditions are really intended to facilitate the conquest of Athens.

Let us, then, approve ourselves men of wisdom; and, fully persuaded of these truths, let us shake off our extravagant and dangerous supineness; let us supply the necessary expenses; let us call on our allies; let us take all possible measures for keeping up a regular army; so that, as he has his force constantly prepared to injure and enslave the Greeks, yours too may be ever ready to protect and assist them. If you depend on occasional detachments you cannot ever expect the least degree of success; you must keep an army constantly on foot, provide for its maintenance, appoint public treasurers, and by all possible means secure your military funds; and while these officers account for all disbursements, let your generals be bound to answer for the conduct of the war. Let these be your measures, these your resolutions, and you will compel Philip to live in the real observance of an equitable peace, and to confine himself to his own kingdom (which is most for our interest), or we shall fight him on equal terms.

If any man thinks that the measures I propose will require great expense, and be attended with much toil and trouble, he thinks justly. Yet let him consider what consequences must attend the state if these measures be neglected, and it will appear that we shall really be gainers by engaging heartily in this cause. Suppose some god should be our surety (for no mortal ought to be relied on in an affair of such moment) that, if we continue quiet, and give up all our interests, he will not at last turn his arms against us; it would yet be shameful; it would (I call all the powers of Heaven to witness!) be unworthy of you, unworthy of the dignity of your country, and the glory of your ancestors, to abandon the rest of Greece to slavery for the sake of private ease. I, for my part, would die rather then propose so mean a conduct: however, if there be any other person who will recommend it, be it so; neglect your defense; give up your interests! But if there be no such counselor; if, on the contrary, we all foresee that the farther this man is suffered to extend his conquests, the more formidable and powerful enemy we must find in him, why this reluctance? why do we delay? or when, my countrymen, will we perform our duty? Must some necessity compel us? What one may call the necessity of freemen not only presses us now, but has long since been felt: that of slaves, it is to be wished, may never approach us. And how do these differ? To a freeman, the disgrace of past misconduct is the most urgent necessity; to a slave stripes and bodily pains. Far be this from us! It ought not to be mentioned.

I would now gladly lay before you the whole

conduct of certain politicians; but I spare them. One thing only I shall observe: the moment that Philip is mentioned there is still one ready to start up, and cry, "What a happiness to live in peace! how grievous the maintenance of a great army! certain persons have designs on our treasury!" Thus they delay their resolutions, and give him full liberty to act as he pleases; hence you gain ease and indulgence for the present (which I fear may at some time prove too dear a purchase); and these men recommend themselves to your favor, and are well paid for their service. But in my opinion there is no need to persuade you to peace, who sit down already thoroughly persuaded. Let it be recommended to him who is committing hostilities; if he can be prevailed on, you are ready to concur. Nor should we think those expenses grievous which our security requires, but the consequences which must arise if such expenses be denied. Then as to plundering our treasury; this must be prevented by intrusting it to proper guardians, not by neglecting our affairs. For my own part, Athenians, I am filled with indignation when I find some persons expressing their impatience, as if our treasures were exposed to plunderers, and yet utterly unaffected at the progress of Philip, who is successively plundering every state of Greece; and this, that he may at last fall with all his fury on you.

What, then, can be the reason, Athenians, that, nothwithstanding all his manifest hostili

ties, all his acts of violence, all the places he
has taken from us, these men will not acknowledge that he has acted unjustly, and that he is
at war with us, but accuse those of embroiling
you in a war who call on you to oppose him
and to check his progress? I shall tell you.
That popular resentment which may arise from
any disagreeable circumstances with which a war
may be attended (and it is necessary, absolutely
necessary that a war should be attended with
many such disagreeable circumstances) they
would cast on your faithful counselors, that
you may pass sentence on them, instead of opposing Philip; and they turn accusers instead
of meeting the punishment due to their present
practises. This is the meaning of their clamors
that certain persons would involve you in a
war: hence have they raised all these cavils
and debates. I know full well that before any
Athenian had ever moved you to declare war
against him, Philip had seized many of our
dominions, and has now sent assistance to the
Cardians. If you are resolved to dissemble your
sense of his hostilities, he would be the weakest
of mankind if he attempted to contradict you.
But suppose he marches directly against us,
what shall we say in that case? He will still
assure us that he is not at war; such were his
professions to the people of Oreum when his
forces were in the heart of their country; and to
those of Pheræ, until the moment that he attacked their walls; and thus he at first amused

the Olynthians, until he had marched his army into their territory. And will you still insist, even in such a case, that they who call on us to defend our country are embroiling us in a war? Then slavery is inevitable. There is no other medium between an obstinate refusal to take arms on your part, and a determined resolution to attack us on the part of our enemy.

Nor is the danger which threatens us the same with that of other people. It is not the conquest of Athens which Philip aims at: no, it is our utter extirpation. He knows full well that slavery is a state you would not, or, if you were inclined, you could not submit to; for sovereignty is become habitual to you. Nor is he ignorant that, at any unfavorable juncture, you have more power to obstruct his enterprises than the whole world besides.

Let us then be assured that we are contending for the very being of our state; let this inspire us with abhorrence of those who have sold themselves to this man, and let them feel the severity of public justice; for it is not possible to conquer our foreign enemy until we have punished those traitors who are serving him within our walls. Else, while we strike on these as so many obstacles, our enemies must necessarily prove superior to us. And whence is it that he dares treat you with insolence (I can not give his present conduct any other name); that he utters menaces against you, while on others he confers acts of kindness (to deceive them at least, if for

no other purpose)? Thus, by heaping favors
on the Thessalians, he has reduced them to their
present slavery. It is not possible to recount
the various artifices by which he abused the
wretched Olynthians, from his first insidious gift
of Potidæa. But now he seduced the Thebans to
his party, by making them masters of Bœotia,
and easing them of a great and grievous war.
And thus, by being gratified in some favorite
point, these people are either involved in calamities known to the whole world, or wait with
submission for the moment when such calamities
are to fall on them. I do not recount all that
you yourselves have lost, Athenians; but in the
very conclusion of the peace, how have you been
deceived? how have you been despoiled? Was
not Phocis, was not Thermopylæ, were not our
Thracian dominions, Doriscum, Serrium, and
even our ally Cersobleptes, all wrested from us?
Is he not at this time in possession of Cardia?
and does he not avow it? Whence is it, I say,
that he treats you in so singular a manner?
Because ours is the only state where there is
allowed full liberty to plead the cause of an
enemy; and the man who sells his country may
harangue securely, at the very time that you
are despoiled of your dominions. It was not
safe to speak for Philip at Olynthus until the
people of Olynthus had been gained by the surrender of Potidæa. In Thessaly it was not safe
to speak for Philip until the Thessalians had
been gained by the expulsion of the tyrants and

the recovery of their rank of amphictyons; nor
could it have been safely attempted at Thebes
before he had restored Bœotia and extirpated
the Phocians. But at Athens, altho he hath
robbed us of Amphipolis and the territory of
Cardia; tho he awes us with his fortifications in
Eubœa; tho he be now on his march to Byzantium; yet his partizans may speak for Philip
without any danger. Hence, some of them, from
the meanest poverty, have on a sudden risen to
affluence; some, from obscurity and disgrace, to
eminence and honor; while you, on the contrary, from glory, have sunk into meanness;
from riches, to poverty; for the riches of a state
I take to be its allies, its credit, its connections,
in all which you are poor. And by your neglect of these, by your utter insensibility to your
wrongs, he is become fortunate and great, the
terror of Greeks and Barbarians; and you abandoned and despised; splendid indeed in the
abundance of your markets; but as to any real
provision for your security, ridiculously defi-
cient.

There are some orators, I find, who view your
interests and their own in a quite different light.
They would persuade you to continue quiet,
whatever injuries are offered to you, they themselves can not be quiet, tho no one offers them
the least injury. When one of these men rises,
I am sure to hear, "What! will you not propose
your decree? will you not venture? No; you
are timid: you want true spirit." I own, in-

deed, I am not, nor would I choose to be, a bold,
an importune, an audacious speaker. And yet,
if I mistake not, I have more real courage than
they who manage your affairs with this rash
hardiness. For he who, neglecting the public interests, is engaged only in trials, in confiscations,
in rewarding, in accusing, doth not act from
any principle of courage, but as he never speaks
but to gain your favor, never proposes measures
that are attended with the least hazard; in this
he has a pledge of his security, and therefore is
he daring. But he who for his country's good
oftentimes opposes your inclinations; who gives
the most salutary, tho not always the most agreeable counsel; who pursues those measures whose
success depends more on fortune than on prudence, and is yet willing to be accountable for
the event; this is the man of courage; this is the
true patriot: not they who, by flattering your
passions, have lost the most important interests
of the state—men whom I am so far from imi-
tating, or deeming citizens of worth, that should
this question be proposed to me, "What services
have you done your country?" tho I might recount the galleys I have fitted out, and the public entertainments I have exhibited and the contributions I have paid, and the captives I have
ransomed, and many like acts of benevolence, I
would yet pass them all by, and only say that
my public conduct hath ever been directly opposite to theirs. I might, like them, have turned
accuser, have distributed rewards and punish-

ments; but this is a part I never assumed; my inclinations were averse; nor could wealth or honors prompt me to it. No; I confine myself to such counsels as have sunk my reputation; but, if pursued, must raise the reputation of my country. Thus much I may be allowed to say without exposing myself to envy. I should not have thought myself a good citizen had I proposed such measures as would have made me the first among my countrymen, but reduced you to the last of states; on the contrary, the faithful minister should raise the glory of his country, and on all occasions advise the most salutary, not the easiest measures. To these nature itself inclines; those are not to be promoted but by the utmost efforts of a wise and faithful counselor.

I have heard it objected, "That indeed I ever speak with reason; yet still this is no more than words—that the state requires something more effectual, some vigorous actions." On which I shall give my sentiments without the least reserve. The sole business of a speaker is, in my opinion, to propose the course you are to pursue. This were easy to be proved. You know that when the great Timotheus moved you to defend the Eubœans against the tyranny of Thebes, he addressed you thus: "What, my countrymen! when the Thebans are actually in the island, are you deliberating what is to be done? what part to be taken? Will you not cover the seas with your navies? Why are you not at the

Piræus? why are you not embarked?'' Thus
Timotheus advised; thus you acted, and success
ensued. But had he spoken with the same spirit,
and had your indolence prevailed, and his advice been rejected, would the state have had the
same success? By no means. And so in the present case: vigor and execution is your part; from
your speakers you are only to expect wisdom and
integrity.

I shall just give the summary of my opinion,
and then descend. You should raise supplies;
you should keep up your present forces, and re-
form whatever abuses may be found in them (not
break them entirely on the first complaint). You
should send ambassadors into all parts, to re-
form, to remonstrate, to exert all their efforts
in the service of the state. But, above all things,
let those corrupt ministers feel the severest punishment; let them, at all times, and in all places,
be the objects of your abhorrence: that wise and
faithful counselors may appear to have con-
sulted their own interests as well as that of
others. If you will act thus, if you will shake
off this indolence, perhaps, even yet, perhaps,
we may promise ourselves some good fortune.
But if you only just exert yourselves in acclamations and applauses, and when anything is
to be done sink again into your supineness, I do
not see how all the wisdom of the world can
save the state from ruin when you deny your
assistance.

III

ON THE CROWN[1]

(330 B.C.)

I BEGIN, men of Athens, by praying to every
god and goddess, that the same good will, which
I have ever cherished toward the commonwealth
and all of you, may be requited to me on the present trial. I pray likewise—and this specially
concerns yourselves, your religion, and your
honor—that the gods may put it in your minds,
not to take counsel of my opponent touching the
manner in which I am to be heard—that would
indeed be cruel!—but of the laws and of your
oath; wherein (besides the other obligations) it
is prescribed that you shall hear both sides alike.
This means, not only that you must pass no pre-
condemnation, not only that you must extend
your good will equally to both, but also that you
must allow the parties to adopt such order and
course of defense as they severally choose and
prefer.

Many advantages hath Æschines over me on
this trial; and two especially, men of Athens.
First, my risk in the contest is not the same. It
is assuredly not the same for me to forfeit your
regard, as for my adversary not to succeed in his
indictment. To me—but I will say nothing un-

---

[1] Delivered in Athens 330 B.C. Translation by Charles R. Kennedy. Abridged. "The most finished," says R. C. Jebb, "the
most splendid and the most pathetic work of ancient eloquence."

toward at the outset of my address. The prosecution, however, is play to him. My second disadvantage is, the natural disposition of mankind to take pleasure in hearing invective and accusation, and to be annoyed by those who praise themselves. To Æschines is assigned the part which gives pleasure; that which is (I may fairly say) offensive to all, is left for me. And if, to escape from this, I make no mention of what I have done, I shall appear to be without defense against his charges, without proof of my claims to honor; whereas, if I proceed to give an account of my conduct and measures, I shall be forced to speak frequently of myself. I will endeavor then to do so with all becoming modesty; what I am driven to do by the necessity of the case, will be fairly chargeable to my opponent, who has instituted such a prosecution.

I think, men of the jury, you will all agree that I, as well as Ctesiphon, am a party to this proceeding, and that it is a matter of no less concern to me. It is painful and grievous to be deprived of anything, especially by the act of one's enemy; but your good will and affection are the heaviest loss, precisely as they are the greatest prize to gain.

Had Æschines confined his charge to the subject of the prosecution, I too would have proceeded at once to my justification of the decree. But since he has wasted no fewer words in the discussion of other matters, in most of them calumniating me, I deem it both necessary and just, men of Athens, to begin by shortly adverting to these points, that none of you may be induced by extraneous arguments to shut your ears against my defense to the indictment.

To all his scandalous abuse of my private life, observe my plain and honest answer. If you know me to be such as he alleged—for I have lived nowhere else but among you—let not my voice be heard, however transcendent my statesmanship! Rise up this instant and condemn me! But if, in your opinion and judgment, I am far better and of better descent than my adversary; if (to speak without offense) I am not inferior, I or mine, to any respectable citizens; then give no credit to him for his other statements—it is plain they were all equally fictions—but to me let the same good will, which you have uniformly exhibited upon many former trials, be manifested now. With all your malice, Æschines, it was very simple to suppose that I should turn from the discussion of measures and policy to notice your scandal. I will do no such thing; I am not so crazed. Your lies and calumnies about my political life I will examine forthwith; for that loose ribaldry I shall have a word hereafter, if the jury desire to hear it.

The crimes whereof I am accused are many and grievous; for some of them the laws enact heavy—most severe penalties. The scheme of this present proceeding includes a combination of spiteful insolence, insult, railing, aspersion, and everything of the kind; while for the said

charges and accusations, if they were true, the
state has not the means of inflicting an adequate
punishment, or anything like it. For it is not
right to debar another of access to the people and
privilege of speech; moreover, to do so by way of
malice and insult—by heaven! is neither honest,
nor constitutional, nor just. If the crimes which
he saw me committing against the state were as
heinous as he so tragically gave out, he ought
to have enforced the penalties of the law against
them at the time; if he saw me guilty of an im-
peachable offense, by impeaching and so bringing me to trial before you; if moving illegal decrees, by indicting me for them. For surely, if
he can prosecute Ctesiphon on my account, he
would not have forborne to indict me myself, had
he thought he could convict me. In short, whatever else he saw me doing to your prejudice,
whether mentioned or not mentioned in his cata-
logue of slander, there are laws for such things,
and punishments, and trials, and judgments,
with sharp and severe penalties; all of which he
might have enforced against me; and had he done
so—had he thus pursued the proper method with
me, his charges would have been consistent with
his conduct. But now he has declined the straightforward and just course, avoided all proofs of
guilt at the time, and after this long interval
gets up, to play his part withal, a heap of accusation, ribaldry and scandal. Then he arraigns
me, but prosecutes the defendant.

What, then, were the statements made by

Æschines, through which everything was lost?
That you should not be alarmed by Philip's having passed Thermopylæ—that all would be as
you desired, if you kept quiet; and in two or
three days you would hear, he was their friend
to whom he had come as an enemy, and that their
enemy to whom he had come as a friend—it was
not words that cemented attachments (such was
his solemn phrase), but identity of interest; and
it was the interest of all alike, Philip, the
Phocians, and you, to be relieved from the harshness and insolence of the Thebans. His assertions were heard by some with pleasure, on account of the hatred which then subsisted against
the Thebans. But what happened directly, almost immediately afterward? The wretched
Phocians were destroyed, their cities demolished;
you that kept quiet, and trusted to Æschines,
were shortly bringing in your effects out of the
country, while Æschines received gold; and yet
more—while you got nothing but your enmity
with the Thebans and Thessalians, Philip won
their gratitude for what he had done.

When you had been deceived by Philip
through the agency of these men, who sold themselves in the embassies, and reported not a word
of truth to you—when the unhappy Phocians
had been deceived and their cities destroyed—
what followed? The despicable Thessalians and
stupid Thebans looked on Philip as a friend, a
benefactor, a savior; he was everything with them
—not a syllable would they hear from any one to

the contrary. You, tho regarding his acts with suspicion and anger, still observed the peace; for you could have done nothing alone. The rest of the Greeks, cheated and disappointed like yourselves, gladly observed the peace, tho they also had in a manner been attacked for a long time. For when Philip was marching about, subduing Illyrians and Triballians and some also of the Greeks, and gaining many considerable accessions of power, and certain citizens of the states (Æschines among them) took advantage of the peace to go there and be corrupted; all people then, against whom he was making such preparations, were attacked.

If they perceived it not, that is another question, no concern of mine. I was forever warning and protesting, both at Athens and wheresoever I was sent. But the states were diseased; one class in their politics and measures being venal and corrupt, while the multitude of private men either had no foresight, or were caught with the bait of present ease and idleness; and all were under some such influence, only they imagined each that the mischief would not approach themselves, but that by the peril of others they might secure their own safety when they chose. The result, I fancy, has been that the people, in return for their gross and unseasonable indolence, have lost their liberty; the statesmen, who imagined they were selling everything but themselves, discovered they had sold themselves first; for, instead of friends, as they were named during the period of bribery, they are now called parasites, and miscreants, and the like befitting names. Justly. For no man, O Athenians, spends money for the traitor's benefit, or, when he has got possession of his purchase, employs the traitor to advise him in future proceedings; else nothing could have been more fortunate than a traitor. But it is not so—it never could be—it is far otherwise! When the aspirant for power has gained his object, he is master also of those that sold it; and then—then, I say, knowing their baseness, he loathes and mistrusts and spurns them.

Consider only—for, tho the time of the events is past, the time for understanding them is ever present to the wise; Lasthenes was called the friend of Philip for a while, until he betrayed Olynthus—Timolaus for a while, until he destroyed Thebes—Eudicus and Simus of Larissa for a while, until they brought Thessaly under Philip's power. Since then the world has become full of traitors, expelled and insulted, and suffering every possible calumny. How fared Aristratus in Sicyon? how Perilaus in Megara? Are they not outcasts? Hence one may evidently see, it is the vigilant defender of his country, the strenuous opponent of such men, who secures to you traitors and hirelings, Æschines, the opportunity of getting bribes: through the number of those that oppose your wishes, you are in safety and in pay; for had it depended on yourselves, you would have perished long ago.

Much more could I say about those transactions, yet methinks too much has been said already. The fault is my adversary's, for having spirted over me the dregs, I may say, of his own wickedness and iniquities, of which I was obliged to clear myself to those who are younger than the events. You, too, have probably been disgusted, who knew this man's venality before I spoke a word. He calls it friendship indeed; and said somewhere in his speech—"the man who reproaches me with the friendship of Alexander." I reproach you with friendship of Alexander! Whence gotten, or how merited? Neither Philip's friend nor Alexander's should I ever call you; I am not so mad—unless we are to call reapers and other hired laborers the friends of those that hire them. That, however, is not so—how could it be? It is nothing of the kind. Philip's hireling I called you once, and Alexander's I call you now. So do all these men. If you disbelieve me, ask them; or rather I will do it for you. Athenians! is Æschines, think ye, the hireling, or the friend of Alexander? You hear what they say!

Philip started, men of Athens, with a great advantage. It happened that among the Greeks —not some, but all alike—there sprang up a crop of traitors and venal wretches, such as in the memory of man had never been before. These he got for his agents and supporters; the Greeks, already ill-disposed and unfriendly to each other, he brought into a still worse state, deceiving this people, making presents to that, corrupting others in every way; and he split them into many parties, when they had all one interest, to prevent his aggrandizement. While the Greeks were all in such a condition—in such ignorance of the gathering and growing mischief—you have to consider, men of Athens, what policy and measures it became the commonwealth to adopt, and of this to receive a reckoning from me; for the man who assumed that post in the administration was I.

But I return to the question—What should the commonwealth, Æschines, have done, when she saw Philip establishing an empire and dominion over Greece? Or what was your statesman to advise or move?—I, a statesman at Athens?—for this is most material—I who knew that from the earliest time until the day of my own mounting the platform, our country had ever striven for precedency and honor and renown, and expended more blood and treasure for the sake of glory and the general weal than the rest of the Greeks had expended on their several interests?—who saw that Philip himself, with whom we were contending, had, in the strife for power and empire, had his eye cut out, his collarbone fractured, his hand and leg mutilated, and was ready and willing to sacrifice any part of his body that fortune chose to take, provided he could live with the remainder in honor and glory? Hardly will any one venture to say this—that it became a man bred at Pella, then an obscure and inconsiderable place, to possess such inborn magnanimity, as to aspire to the mastery of Greece and form the project in his mind, while you, who were Athenians, day after day in speeches and in dramas reminded of the virtue of your ancestors, should have been so naturally base, as of your own free will and accord to surrender to Philip the liberty of Greece. No man will say this!

The only course then that remained was a just resistance to all his attacks upon you. Such course you took from the beginning, properly and becomingly; and I assisted by motions and counsels during the period of my political life:— I acknowledge it. But what should I have done? Was it meet that any of the Greeks should rise up to prevent these proceedings, or not? If not —if Greece was to present the spectacle (as it is called) of a Mysian prey, while Athenians had life and being, then I have exceeded my duty in speaking on the subject—the commonwealth has exceeded her duty, which followed my counsels— I admit that every measure has been a misdeed, a blunder of mine. But if some one ought to have arisen to prevent these things, who but the Athenian people should it have been? Such then was the policy which I espoused. I saw him reducing all men to subjection, and I opposed him; I continued warning and exhorting you not to make these sacrifices to Philip.

When Philip therefore was driven out of Eubœa, with arms by you, with counsels and decrees—

tho some persons there should burst!—by me, he sought some new position of attack upon Athens. Seeing that we use more foreign corn than any people, and wishing to command the passage of the corn-trade, he advanced to Thrace; the Byzantines being his allies, he first required them to join in the war against you, and when they refused, saying (truly enough) that they had not made alliance on such terms, he threw up intrenchments before the city, planted batteries, and laid siege to it. What course hereupon it became you to take, I will not ask again; it is manifest to all. But who was it that succored the Byzantines, and rescued them? who prevented the alienation of the Hellespont at that crisis? You, men of Athens. When I say you, I mean the commonwealth. But who advised, framed, executed the measures of state, devoted himself wholly and unreservedly to the public business?—I!—What benefits thence accrued to all, you need no further to be told; you have learned by experience. For the war which then sprang up, besides that it brought honor and renown, kept you in a cheaper and more plentiful supply of all the necessaries of life than does the present peace, which these worthies maintain to their country's prejudice in the hope of something to come. Perish such hope! Never may they share the blessings for which you men of honest wishes pray to the gods, or communicate their own principles to you!

Thus the saving of Chersonesus and Byzantium, the preventing Philip's conquest of the Hellespont, and the honors therefore bestowed on this country, were the effects of my policy and administration; and more than this—they proved to all mankind the generosity of Athens and the baseness of Philip. He, the ally and friend of the Byzantines, was before all eyes besieging them—what could be more shameful or outrageous?—You, who might justly on many grounds have reproached them for wrongs done you in former times, instead of bearing malice and abandoning the oppressed, appeared as their deliverers; conduct which procured you glory, good-will, honors from all men. That you have crowned many of your statesmen, every one knows; but through what other person (I mean what minister or orator), besides myself, the commonwealth has been crowned, no one can say.

Well then, men of Athens—when the Lacedæmonians had the empire of land and sea, and held the country round Attica by governors and garrisons, Eubœa, Tanagra, all Bœotia, Megara, Ægina, Cleonæ, the other islands; when our state possessed neither ships nor walls; you marched out to Haliartus, and again not many days after to Corinth; albeit the Athenians of that time had many causes of resentment against both Corinthians and Thebans for their acts in the Decelean war; but they showed no resentment, none. And yet neither of these steps took they, Æschines, for benefactors, nor were they blind to the danger; but they would not for such reasons abandon people who sought their protection; for the sake of renown and glory they willingly exposed themselves to peril; just and noble was their resolve! For to all mankind the end of life is death, tho one keep one's self shut up in a closet; but it becomes brave men to strive always for honor, with good hope before them, and to endure courageously whatever the Deity ordains.

Thus did your ancestors, thus the elder among yourselves. For, tho the Lacedæmonians were neither friends nor benefactors, but had done many grievous injuries to our state, yet when the Thebans, victorious at Leuctra, sought their destruction, you prevented it, not fearing the power and reputation then possessed by the Thebans, nor reckoning up the merits of those whom you were about to fight for. And so you demonstrated to all the Greeks, that, however any people may offend you, you reserve your anger against them for other occasions; but should their existence or liberty be imperiled, you will not resent your wrongs or bring them into account.

I must return to the next in date of my political acts; and here again consider what was most beneficial for the state. I saw, men of Athens, that your navy was decaying, and that, while the rich were getting off with small payments, citizens of moderate or small fortunes were losing their substance, and the state, by reason thereof, missing her opportunities of action. I, therefore, proposed a law, by which I compelled the one class (the rich) to perform their duty, and stopped the oppression of the poor; and—what was most useful to the country—I caused her preparations to be made in time. And being indicted for it, I appeared on the charge before you, and was acquitted; and the prosecutor did not get his portion of the votes. But what sums, think ye, the chief men of the boards, or those in the second and third degrees, offered me, first, not to propose that law, secondly, when I had recorded it, to drop it on the abatement-oath? Such sums, men of Athens, as I should be afraid to tell you. And no wonder they did so; for under the former laws they might divide the charge between sixteen, spending little or nothing themselves, and grinding down the needy citizens; whereas under my law every one had to pay a sum proportioned to his means, and there was a captain for two ships, where before there was a partner with fifteen others for one ship; for they were calling themselves not captains any longer, but partners. They would have given anything to get these regulations annulled, and not be obliged to perform their duties.

Why then, wretched man, do you play the pettifogger? Why manufacture arguments? Why don't you take hellebore[1] for your malady? Are you not ashamed to bring on a cause for spite, and not for any offense?—to alter some laws, and to garble others, the whole of which should in

---

[1] Hellebore, tho a poison, was used by the Greeks in mild doses to clear the brain and cure insanity.

justice be read to persons sworn to decide according to the laws? And you that act thus describe the qualities which belong to a friend of the people, as if you had ordered a statue according to contract, and received it without having what the contract required; or as if friends of the people were known by words, and not by acts and measures! And you bawl out, regardless of decency, a sort of cart-language, applicable to yourself and your race, not to me.

Again, men of Athens—I conceive abuse to differ from accusation in this, that accusation has to do with offenses for which the laws provide penalties, abuse with the scandal which enemies speak against each other according to their humor. And I believe your ancestors built these courts, not that we should assemble you here and bring forth the secrets of private life for mutual reproach, but to give us the means of convicting persons guilty of crimes against the state. Æschines knew this as well as I, and yet he chose to rail rather than to accuse.

Even in this way he must take as much as he gives; but before I enter upon such matters, let me ask him one question—Should one call you the state's enemy, or mine, Æschines? Mine, of course. Yet, where you might, for any offense, which I committed, have obtained satisfaction for the people according to the laws, you neglected it—at the audit, on the indictments and other trials; but where I in my own person am safe on every account, by the laws, by time, by prescription, by many previous judgments on every point, by my never having been convicted of a public offense—and where the country must share, more or less, in the repute of measures which were her own—here it is you have encountered me. See if you are not the people's enemy, while you pretend to be mine!

I am at no loss for materials concerning you and your family, but am in doubt what to mention first—whether how your father Tromes, being servant to Elpias, who kept a reading-school in the temple of Theseus, wore a weight of fetters and a collar; or how your mother, by her morning spousals in the cottage by Hero Calamites, reared up you, the beautiful statue, the eminent third-rate actor!—But all know these things without my telling—Or how the galley-piper Phormio, the slave of Dion of Phrearrii, removed her from that honorable employment. But, by Jupiter and the gods! I fear, in saying what is proper about you, I may be thought to have chosen topics unbecoming to myself. All this therefore, I shall pass by, and commence with the acts of his own life; for indeed he came not of common parents, but of such as are execrated by the people. Very lately—lately do I say?—it is but yesterday that he has become both an Athenian and an orator—adding two syllables, he converted his father from Tromes to Atrometus, and dignified his mother by the name of Glaucothea, who (as every one knows) was called

Empusa[1]; having got that title (it is plain) from her doing and submitting to anything—how else could she have got it? However, you are so ungrateful and wicked by nature, that after being raised through the people from servitude to freedom, from beggary to affluence, instead of returning their kindness, you work against them as a hireling politician.

That he should cooperate openly with Philip before the war, was shocking—O heaven and earth! could it be otherwise?—against his country! Yet allow him if you please, allow him this. But when the ships had openly been made prize, Chersonesus was ravaged, the man was marching against Attica, matters were no longer doubtful, war had begun—nothing that he ever did for you can this malicious iambic-mouther show—not a resolution has Æschines, great or small, concerning the interests of the state. If he asserts it, let him prove it now while my waterglass[2] is running. But there is none. He is reduced to an alternative;—either he had no fault to find with my measures, and therefore moved none against them; or he sought the good of the enemy, and therefore would not propose any better.

[1] This denotes a frightful specter or hobgoblin. According to Aristophanes (Frogs, 283) it could change itself into various shapes.—Kennedy.

[2] The Athenians, to prevent the parties from saying more than was necessary, timed them by a glass in which water trickled through a narrow tube like sand in one of our minute glasses.—Kennedy.

Did he abstain from speaking as well as moving, when any mischief was to be done to you? Why, no one else could speak a word. Other things, it appears, the country could endure, and he could accomplish without detection; but one last act he achieved, O Athenians, which crowned all he had done before; on which he lavished that multitude of words, recounting the decrees against the Amphissian Locrians, in hopes of distorting the truth. But the thing admits it not. No! never will you wash yourself clean from your performances there—talk as long as you will!

In your presence, men of Athens, I invoke all the gods and goddesses to whom the Attic territory belongs, and Pythian Apollo the Father-god of our state; and I implore them all! As I shall declare the truth to you, as I declared it in your assembly at the time, the very moment I saw this wretch putting his hand to the work—for I perceived, instantly perceived it—so may they grant me favor and protection! If from malice or personal rivalry I bring a false charge against my opponent, may they cut me off from every blessing!

But wherefore this imprecation, this solemn assurance? Because, tho I have documents lying in the public archives, from which I shall clearly prove my assertions, tho I know you remember the facts, I fear this man may be considered unequal to the mischiefs which he has wrought; as before happened, when he caused the destruction of the unhappy Phocians by his false reports to you.

The Amphissian War, I say—which brought Philip to Elatea, which caused him to be chosen general of the Amphictyons, which ruined everything in Greece—was this man's contrivance. He is the single author of all our heaviest calamities. I protested at the time, and cried out in the assembly—"You are bringing a war, Æschines, into Attica, an Amphictyonic war"— but his packed party would not let me be heard; the rest wondered, and supposed that I was bringing an idle charge against him out of personal enmity. However, the real character of those transactions, the purpose for which they were got up, the manner in which they were accomplished, hear ye now, men of Athens, as ye were prevented then. You will see that the thing was well concerted, and it will help you much to get a knowledge of public affairs, and what craftiness there was in Philip you will observe.

Philip could neither finish nor get rid of the war with Athens, unless he made the Thebans and Thessalians her enemies. Tho your generals fought against him without fortune or skill, yet from the war itself and the cruisers he suffered infinite damage. He could neither export any of the produce of his country, nor import what he needed. He was not then superior to you at sea, nor able to reach Attica, unless the Thessalians followed him and the Thebans gave him a passage; so that, while he overcame in war

the generals whom you sent out—such as they
were—I say nothing about that—he found himself distressed by the difference of your local
position and means. Should he urge either Thessalians or Thebans to march in his own quarrel
against you, none, he thought, would attend to
him : but should he, under the pretense of taking
up their common cause, be elected general, he
trusted partly by deceit and partly by persuasion to gain his ends more easily. He sets to
work therefore—observe how cleverly—to get the
Amphictyons into a war, and create a disturb-
ance in the congress. For this he thought they
would immediately want him. Now, if any of
the presbyters commissioned by himself or any
of his allies brought it forward, he imagined
that both Thebans and Thessalians would sus-
pect the thing, and would all be on their guard ;
whereas, if the agent were an Athenian and commissioned by you his opponents, it would easily
pass unnoticed. An thus it turned out.

How did he effect his purpose? He hires the
prosecutor. No one (I believe) was aware of the
thing or attending to it, and so—just as these
things are usually done at Athens—Æschines
was proposed for Pylæan deputy, three or four
held up their hands for him, and his election was
declared. When clothed with the dignity of the
state he arrived among the Amphictyons, dis-
missing and disregarding all besides, he hastened
to execute what he was hired for. He makes up
a pretty speech and story, showing how the Cir-

rhæan plain came to be consecrated; reciting this to the presbyters, men unused to speeches and unsuspicious of any consequences.

The mention of this man's treasonable acts brings me to the part which I have myself taken in opposition to him. It is fair you should hear my account of it for many reasons, but chiefly, men of Athens, because it would be a shame, when I have undergone the toil of exertions on your behalf, that you should not endure the bare recital of them.

When I say that the Thebans, and I may add the Athenians, were so led away by Philip's partizans and the corrupt men of either state, as to disregard and take no precaution against a danger which menaced both, and required the utmost precaution (I mean the suffering Philip's power to increase), and were readily disposed to enmity and strife with each other; I was constantly watchful to prevent it, not only because in my own judgment I deemed such vigilance expedient, but knowing that Aristophon, and again Eubulus, had all along desired to bring about that union, and, while they were frequently opposed upon other matters, were always agreed upon this. Men whom in their lifetime—you reptile!—you pestered with flattery, yet see not that you are accusing them in their graves: for the Theban policy that you reproach me with is a charge less affecting me than them, who approved that alliance before I did. But I must return.—I say, when Æschines had excited the

war in Amphissa, and his coadjutors had helped
to establish enmity with Thebes, Philip marched
against us—that was the object for which these
persons embroiled the states—and had we not
roused up a little in time, we could never have recovered ourselves: so far had these men carried
matters.

Now, Æschines, how would you have me describe you, and how myself, upon that day?
Shall I call myself Batalus, your nickname of
reproach, and you not even a hero of the common
sort, but one of those upon the stage, Cresphontes
or Creon, or the Œnomaus whom you execrably
murdered once at Colyttus? Well; upon that
occasion I the Batalus of Pæania was more serviceable to the state than you the Œnomaus of
Cothocidæ. You were of no earthly use; I did
everything which became a good citizen.

Had I attempted to say, that I instructed you
in sentiments worthy of your ancestors, there is
not a man who would not justly rebuke me.
What I declare is, that such principles are your
own; I show that before my time such was the
spirit of the commonwealth; tho certainly in
the execution of the particular measures I claim
a share also for myself. The prosecutor, ar-
raigning the whole proceedings, and embittering
you against me as the cause of our alarms and
dangers, in his eagerness to deprive me of honor
for the moment, robs you of the eulogies that
should endure for ever. For should you, under
a disbelief in the wisdom of my policy convict

the defendant, you will appear to have done
wrong not to have suffered what befel you by
the cruelty of fortune. But never, never can you
have done wrong, O Athenians, in undertaking
the battle for the freedom and safety of all! I
swear it by your forefathers—those that met the
peril at Marathon, those that took the field at
Platæa, those in the sea-fight at Salamis, and
those at Artemisium, and many other brave men
who repose in the public monuments, all of whom
alike, as being worthy of the same honor, the
country buried, Æschines, not only the successful or victorious! Justly! For the duty of
brave men has been done by all: their fortune
has been such as the Deity assigned to each.

Accursed scribbler! you, to deprive me of the
approbation and affection of my countrymen,
speak of trophies and battles and ancient deeds,
with none of which had this present trial the
least concern; but I!—O you third-rate actor!—
I, that rose to counsel the state how to maintain
her preeminence! in what spirit was I to mount
the hustings? In the spirit of one having unworthy counsel to offer?—I should have deserved
to perish! You yourselves, men of Athens, may
not try private and public causes on the same
principles: the compacts of every-day life you
are to judge of by particular laws and circumstances; the measures of statesmen, by reference to the dignity of your ancestors. And
if you think it your duty to act worthily of them,
you should every one of you consider, when you

come into court to decide public questions, that together with your staff and ticket the spirit of the commonwealth is delivered to you.

Athenians, you have had many great and renowned orators before me; the famous Callistratus, Aristophon, Cephalus, Thrasybulus, hundreds of others, yet none of them ever thoroughly devoted himself to any measure of state: for instance, the mover of a resolution would not be ambassador; the ambassador would not move a resolution; each one left for himself some relief, and also, should anything happen, an excuse. How then—it may be said—did you so far surpass others in might and boldness as to do everything yourself? I don't say that: but such was my conviction of the danger impending over us, that I considered it left no room or thought for individual security; a man should have been only too happy to perform his duty without neglect. As to myself I was persuaded, perhaps foolishly, yet I was persuaded, that none would move better resolutions than myself, none would execute them better, none as ambassador would show more zeal and honesty. Therefore I undertook every duty myself.

Through my policy, which he arraigns, instead of the Thebans invading this country with Philip, as all expected, they joined our ranks and prevented him;—instead of the war being in Attica, it took place seven hundred furlongs from the city on the confines of Bœotia;—instead of corsairs issuing from Eubœa to plunder us, At-

tica was in peace on the coast-side during the
whole war;—instead of Philip being master of
the Hellespont by taking Byzantium, the Byzantines were our auxiliaries against him. Does
this computation of services, think you, resemble
the casting of accounts? Or should we strike
these out on a balance, and not look that they
be kept in everlasting remembrance? I will not
set down, that of the cruelty, remarkable in cases
where Philip got people all at once into his
power, others have had the trial; while of the
generosity, which, casting about for his future
purposes, he assumed toward Athens, you have
happily enjoyed the fruits. I pass that by.

If you talk about just conditions with the Thebans, Æschines, or with the Byzantines or Eubœans, or discuss now the question of equal terms,
first I say—you are ignorant that of those galleys formerly which defended Greece, being three
hundred in number, our commonwealth furnished two hundred, and never (as it seemed)
thought herself injured by having done so, never
prosecuted those who advised it or expressed any
dissatisfaction—shame on her if she had!—but
was grateful to the gods, that, when a common
danger beset the Greeks, she alone furnished
double what the rest did for the preservation of
all. Besides, it is but a poor favor you do your
countrymen by calumniating me. For what is
the use of telling us now what we should have
done? Why, being in the city and present, did
you not make your proposals then; if indeed they

were practicable at a crisis, when we had to accept not what we liked but what the circumstances allowed? Remember, there was one ready to bid against us, to welcome eagerly those that we rejected, and give money into the bargain.

But if I am accused for what I have actually done, how would it have been, if, through my hard bargaining, the states had gone off and attached themselves to Philip, and he had become master at the same time of Eubœa, Thebes, and Byzantium? What, think ye, these impious men would have said or done? Said doubtless, that the states were abandoned—that they wished to join us and were driven away—that he had got command of the Hellespont by the Byzantines, and become master of the corn-trade of Greece—that a heavy neighbor-war had by means of the Thebans been brought into Attica—that the sea had become unnavigable by the excursion of pirates from Eubœa! All this would they have said sure enough, and a great deal besides. A wicked, wicked thing, O Athenians, is a calumniator always, every way spiteful and faultfinding. But this creature is a reptile by nature, that from the beginning never did anything honest or liberal; a very ape of a tragedian, village Œnomaus, counterfeit orator! What advantage has your eloquence been to your country? Now do you speak to us about the past? As if a physician should visit his patients, and not order or prescribe anything to cure the disease, but on the death of any one, when the last ceremonies were performing, should follow him to the grave and expound, how, if the poor fellow had done this and that, he never would have died! Idiot, do you speak now?

Even the defeat—if you exult in that which should make you groan, you accursed one!—by nothing that I have done will it appear to have befallen us. Consider it thus, O Athenians. From no embassy, on which I was commissioned by you, did I ever come away defeated by the ambassadors of Philip—neither from Thessaly, nor from Ambracia, nor from the kings of Thrace, nor from Byzantium, nor from any other place, nor on the last recent occasion from Thebes; but where his ambassadors were vanquished in argument, he came with arms and carried the day. And for this you call me to account; and are not ashamed to jeer the same person for cowardice, whom you require single-handed to overcome the might of Philip—and that, too, by words! For what else had I at my command? Certainly not the spirit of each individual, nor the fortune of the army, nor the conduct of the war, for which you would make me accountable; such a blunderer are you!

Yet understand me. Of what a statesman may be responsible for I allow the utmost scrutiny; I deprecate it not. What are his functions? To observe things in the beginning, to foresee and foretell them to others,—this I have done: again; wherever he finds delays, backwardness, ignorance, jealousies, vices inherent and unavoidable in all communities, to contract them into the narrowest compass, and on the other hand, to promote unanimity and friendship and zeal in the discharge of duty. All this, too, I have performed; and no one can discover the least neglect on my part. Ask any man, by what means Philip achieved most of his successes, and you will be told, by his army, and by his bribing and corrupting men in power. Well; your forces were not under my command or control; so that I can not be questioned for anything done in that department. But by refusing the price of corruption I have overcome Philip; for as the offerer of a bribe, if it be accepted, has vanquished the taker, so the person who refuses it and is not corrupted has vanquished the person offering. Therefore is the commonwealth undefeated as far as I am concerned.

For my part, I regard any one, who reproaches his fellow man with fortune, as devoid of sense. He that is best satisfied with his condition, he that deems his fortune excellent, can not be sure that it will remain so until the evening: how then can it be right to bring it forward, or upbraid another man with it? As Æschines, however, has on this subject (besides many others) expressed himself with insolence, look, men of Athens, and observe how much more truth and humanity there shall be in my discourse upon fortune than in his.

I hold the fortune of our commonwealth to be

good, and so I find the oracles of Dodonæan
Jupiter and Phythian Apollo declaring to us.
The fortune of all mankind, which now prevails,
I consider cruel and dreadful: for what Greek,
what barbarian, has not in these times experienced a multitude of evils? That Athens chose
the noblest policy, that she fares better than
those very Greeks who thought, if they abandoned us, they should abide in prosperity, I
reckon as part of her good fortune; if she suffered reverses, if all happened not to us as we
desired, I conceive she has had that share of the
general fortune which fell to our lot. As to my
fortune (personally speaking) or that of any individual among us, it should, as I conceive, be
judged of in connection with personal matters.
Such is my opinion upon the subject of fortune,
a right and just one, as it appears to me, and I
think you will agree with it. Æschines says that
my individual fortune is paramount to that of
the commonwealth, the small and mean to the
good and great. How can this possibly be?

However, if you are determined, Æschines, to
scrutinize my fortune, compare it with your own,
and, if you find my fortune better than yours,
cease to revile it. Look then from the very beginning. And I pray and entreat that I may not
be condemned for bad taste. I don't think any
person wise, who insults poverty, or who prides
himself on having been bred in affluence: but by
the slander and malice of this cruel man I am
forced into such a discussion; which I will con-

duct with all the moderation which circumstances allow.

I had the advantage, Æschines, in my boyhood of going to proper schools, and having such allowance as a boy should have who is to do nothing mean from indigence. Arrived at man's estate, I lived suitably to my breeding; was choirmaster, ship-commander, rate-payer; backward in no acts of liberality public or private, but making myself useful to the commonwealth and to my friends. When I entered upon state affairs, I chose such a line of politics, that both by my country and many people of Greece I have been crowned many times, and not even you my enemies venture to say that the line I chose was not honorable. Such then has been the fortune of my life: I could enlarge upon it, but I forbear, lest what I pride myself in should give offense.

But you, the man of dignity, who spit upon others, look what sort of fortune is yours compared with mine. As a boy you were reared in abject poverty, waiting with your father in his school, grinding the ink, sponging the benches, sweeping the room, doing the duty of a menial rather than a freeborn man. After you were grown up, you attended your mother in the initiations, reading her books and helping in all the ceremonies; at night wrapping the noviciates in fawn-skin, swilling, purifying, and scouring them with clay and bran, raising them after the lustration, and bidding them say, "Bad I have

scaped, and better I have found''; priding yourself that no one ever howled so lustily—and I
believe him! for don't suppose that he who
speaks so loud is not a splendid howler! In the
daytime you led ycur noble orgiasts, crowned
with fennel and poplar, through the highways,
squeezing the big-cheeked serpents, and lifting
them over your head, and shouting Evœ Sabœ,
and capering to the words Hyes Attes, Attes
Hyes, saluted by the beldames as Leader, Con-
ductor, Chest-bearer, Fan-bearer, and the like,
getting as your reward tarts and biscuits and
rolls; for which any man might well bless himself and his fortune!

When you were enrolled among your fellow
townsmen—by what means I stop not to inquire
—when you were enrolled, however, you immediately selected the most honorable of employ-
ments, that of clerk and assistant to our petty
magistrates. From this you were removed after
a while, having done yourself all that you charge
others with; and then, sure enough, you dis-
graced not your antecedents by your subsequent
life, but hiring yourself to those ranting players,
as they were called, Simylus and Socrates, you
acted third parts, collecting figs and grapes and
olives like a fruiterer from other men's farms,
and getting more from them than from the playing, in which the lives of your whole company
were at stake; for there was an implacable and
incessant war between them and the audience,
from whom you received so many wounds, that

no wonder you taunt as cowards people inexperienced in such encounters.

But passing over what may be imputed to poverty, I will come to the direct charges against your character. You espoused such a line of politics (when at last you thought of taking to them) that, if your country prospered, you lived the life of a hare, fearing and trembling and ever expecting to be scourged for the crimes of which your conscience accused you; tho all have seen how bold you were during the misfortunes of the rest. A man who took courage at the death of a thousand citizens—what does he deserve at the hands of the living? A great deal more than I could say about him I shall omit; for it is not all I can tell of his turpitude and infamy which I ought to let slip from my tongue, but only what is not disgraceful to myself to mention.

Contrast now the circumstances of your life and mine, gently and with temper, Æschines; and then ask these people whose fortune they would each of them prefer. You taught reading, I went to school; you performed initiations, I received them; you danced in the chorus, I furnished it; you were assembly clerk, I was a speaker; you acted third parts, I heard you; you broke down, and I hissed; you have worked as a statesman for the enemy, I for my country. I pass by the rest; but this very day I am on my probation for a crown, and am acknowledged to be innocent of all offense; while you are already judged to be a pettifogger, and the question is, whether you shall continue that trade, or at once be silenced by not getting a fifth part of the votes. A happy fortune, do you see, you have enjoyed, that you should denounce mine as miserable!

I will have done then with private topics, but say another word or two upon public. If you can mention, Æschines, a single man under the sun, whether Greek or barbarian, who has not suffered by Philip's power formerly and Alexander's now, well and good; I concede to you, that my fortune, or misfortune (if you please), has been the cause of everything. But if many that never saw me or heard my voice have been grievously afflicted, not individuals only but whole cities and nations; how much juster and fairer is it to consider, that to the common fortune apparently of all men, to a tide of events overwhelming and lamentable, these disasters are to be attributed. You, disregarding all this, accuse me whose ministry has been among my countrymen, knowing all the while, that a part (if not the whole) of your calumny falls upon the people, and yourself in particular. For if I assumed the sole and absolute direction of our counsels, it was open to you the other speakers to accuse me; but if you were constantly present in all the assemblies, if the state invited public discussion of what was expedient, and if these measures were then believed by all to be the best, and especially by you (for certainly from no good-will did you leave me in possession of hopes and admiration and honors, all of which attended on my policy, but doubtless because you were compelled by the truth and had nothing better to advise); is it not iniquitous and monstrous to complain now of measures, than which you could suggest none better at the time?

I should conclude, Æschines, that you undertook this cause to exhibit your eloquence and strength of lungs, not to obtain satisfaction for any wrong. But it is not the language of an orator, Æschines, that has any value, nor yet the tone of his voice, but his adopting the same views with the people, and his hating and loving the same persons that his country does. He that is thus minded will say everything with loyal intention; he that courts persons from whom the commonwealth apprehends danger to herself, rides not on the same anchorage with the people, and, therefore, has not the same expectation of safety. But—do you see?—I have; for my objects are the same with those of my countrymen; I have no interest separate or distinct. Is that so with you? How can it be—when immediately after the battle you went as ambassador to Philip, who was at that period the author of your country's calamities, notwithstanding that you had before persisted in refusing that office, as all men know?

And who is it that deceives the state? Surely the man who speaks not what he thinks. On whom does the crier pronounce a curse? Surely on such a man. What greater crime can an orator be charged with than that his opinions and his language are not the same? Such is found to be your character. And yet you open your mouth, and dare to look these men in the faces! Do you think they don't know you?—or are sunk in such slumber and oblivion, as not to remember the speeches which you delivered in the assembly, cursing and swearing that you had nothing to do with Philip, and that I brought that charge against you out of personal enmity without foundation? No sooner came the news of the battle, than you forgot all that; you acknowledge and avowed that between Philip and yourself there subsisted a relation of hospitality and friendship —new names these for your contract of hire. For upon what plea of equality or justice could Æschines, son of Glaucothea, the timbrel player, be the friend or acquaintance of Philip? I cannot see. No! You were hired to ruin the interests of your countrymen; and yet, tho you have been caught yourself in open treason, and informed against yourself after the fact, you revile and reproach me for things which you will find any man is chargeable with sooner than I.

Many great and glorious enterprises has the commonwealth, Æschines, undertaken and succeeded in through me; and she did not forget them. Here is the proof—On the election of a person to speak the funeral oration immediately after the event, you were proposed, but the people would not have you, notwithstanding your

fine voice, nor Demades, tho he had just made
the peace, nor Hegemon, nor any other of your
party—but me. And when you and Pythocles
came forward in a brutal and shameful manner (O merciful Heaven!) and urged the same
accusations against me which you now do, and
abused me, they elected me all the more. The
reason—you are not ignorant of it—yet I will
tell you. The Athenians knew as well the loyalty and zeal with which I conducted their affairs, as the dishonesty of you and your party;
for what you denied upon oath in our prosperity,
you confessed in the misfortunes of the repub-
lic. They considered, therefore, that men who
got security for their politics by the public disasters had been their enemies long before, and
were then avowedly such. They thought it right
also, that the person who was to speak in honor
of the fallen and celebrate their valor should not
have sat under the same roof or at the same table
with their antagonists; that he should not revel
there and sing a pæan over the calamities of
Greece in company with their murderers, and
then come here and receive distinction; that he
should not with his voice act the mourner of their
fate, but that he should lament over them with
his heart. This they perceived in themselves
and in me, but not in any of you; therefore, they
elected me, and not you. Nor, while the people
felt thus, did the fathers and brothers of the
deceased, who were chosen by the people to perform their obsequies, feel differently. For hav-

ing to order the funeral banquet (according to custom) at the house of the nearest relative to the deceased, they ordered it at mine. And with reason; because, tho each to his own was nearer of kin than I was, none was so near to them all collectively. He that had the deepest interest in their safety and success had upon their mournful disaster the largest share of sorrow for them all.

Of this base and infamous conspiracy and profligacy—or rather, O Athenians, if I am to speak in earnest, of this betrayal of Grecian liberty—Athens is by all mankind acquitted, owing to my counsels; and I am acquitted by you. Then do you ask me, Æschines, for what merit I claim to be honored? I will tell you. Because, while all the statesmen in Greece, beginning with yourself, have been corrupted formerly by Philip and now by Alexander, me neither opportunity, nor fair speeches, nor large promises, nor hope, nor fear, nor anything else could tempt or induce to betray aught that I considered just and beneficial to my country. Whatever I have advised my fellow citizens, I have never advised like you men, leaning as in a balance to the side of profit; all my proceedings have been those of a soul upright, honest, and incorrupt; entrusted with affairs of greater magnitude than any of my contemporaries, I have administered them all honestly and faithfully. Therefore do I claim to be honored.

These and the like measures, Æschines, are

what become an honorable citizen (by their success—O earth and heaven!—we should have been the greatest of people incontestably, and deserved to be so; even under their failure the result is glory, and no one blames Athens or her policy; all condemn fortune that so ordered things); but never will he desert the interests of the commonwealth, nor hire himself to her adversaries, and study the enemy's advantage instead of his country's; nor on a man who has courage to advise and propose measures worthy of the state, and resolution to persevere in them, will he cast an evil eye, and, if any one privately offends him, remember and treasure it up; no, nor keep himself in a criminal and treacherous retirement, as you so often do. There is indeed a retirement just and beneficial to the state, such as you, the bulk of my countrymen, innocently enjoy; that however is not the retirement of Æschines; far from it. Withdrawing himself from public life when he pleases, (and that is often) he watches for the moment when you are tired of a constant speaker, or when some reverse of fortune has befallen you, or anything untoward has happened (and many are the casualties of human life); at such a crisis he springs up an orator, rising from his retreat like a wind; in full voice, with words and phrases collected, he rolls them out audibly and breathlessly, to no advantage or good purpose whatsoever, but to the detriment of some or other of his fellow citizens and to the general disgrace.

Yet from this labor and diligence, Æschines, if it proceeded from an honest heart, solicitous for your country's welfare, the fruits should have been rich and noble and profitable to all —alliances of states, supplies of money, conveniences of commerce, enactment of useful laws, opposition to our declared enemies. All such things were looked for in former times; and many opportunities did the past afford for a good man and true to show himself; during which time you are nowhere to be found, neither first, second, third, fourth, fifth, nor sixth—not in any rank at all—certainly on no service by which your country was exalted. For what alliance has come to the state by your procurement? What succors, what acquisition of good will or credit? What embassy or agency is there of yours, by which the reputation of the country has been increased? What concern domestic, Hellenic, or foreign, of which you have had the management, has improved under it? What galleys? what ammunition? what arsenals? what repair of walls? what cavalry? What in the world are you good for? What assistance in money have you ever given, either to the rich or the poor, out of public spirit or liberality? None. But, good sir, if there is nothing of this, there is at all events zeal and loyalty. Where? when? You infamous fellow! Even at a time when all who ever spoke upon the platform gave something for the public safety, and last Aristonicus gave the sum which he had amassed to retrieve his franchise, you

neither came forward nor contributed a mite
—not from inability—no, for you have inherited
above five talents from Philo, your wife's father,
and you had a subscription of two talents from
the chairmen of the boards for what you did to
cut up the navy law. But, that I may not go
from one thing to another and lose sight of the
question, I pass this by. That it was not poverty
prevented your contributing, already appears; it
was, in fact, your anxiety to do nothing against
those to whom your political life is subservient.
On what occasions then do you show your spirit?
When do you shine out? When aught is to be
spoken against your countrymen!—then it is
you who are splendid in voice, perfect in memory, an admirable actor, a tragic Theocrines.

You mention the good men of olden times; and
you are right so to do. Yet it is hardly fair, O
Athenians, that he should get the advantage of
that respect which you have for the dead, to
compare and contrast me with them,—me who
am living among you; for what mortal is ignorant, that toward the living there exists always
more or less of ill will, whereas the dead are no
longer hated even by an enemy? Such being
human nature, am I to be tried and judged by
the standard of my predecessors? Heaven forbid! It is not just nor equitable, Æschines. Let
me be compared with you, or any persons you
like of your party who are still alive. And consider this—whether it is more honorable and
better for the state, that because of the services

of a former age, prodigious tho they are beyond all power of expression, those of the present generation should be unrequited and spurned, or that all who give proof of their good intentions should have their share of honor and regard from the people? Yet, indeed—if I must say so much—my politics and principles, if considered fairly, will be found to resemble those of the illustrious ancients, and to have had the same objects in view, while yours resemble those of their calumniators; for it is certain there were persons in those times, who ran down the living, and praised people dead and gone, with a malignant purpose like yourself.

You say that I am nothing like the ancients. Are you like them, Æschines? Is your brother, or any of our speakers? I assert that none is. But pray, my good fellow (that I may give you no other name), try the living with the living and with his competitors, as you would in all cases—poets, dancers, athletes. Philammon did not, because he was inferior to Glaucus of Carystus and some other champions of a bygone age, depart uncrowned from Olympia, but, because he beat all who entered the ring against him, was crowned and proclaimed conqueror. So I ask you to compare me with the orators of the day, with yourself, with any one you like; I yield to none. When the commonwealth was at liberty to choose for her advantage, and patriotism was a matter of emulation, I showed myself a better counselor than any, and every act of state was pursuant to my decrees and laws and negotiations; none of your party was to be seen, unless you had to do the Athenians a mischief. After that lamentable occurrence, when there was a call no longer for advisers, but for persons obedient to command, persons ready to be hired against their country and willing to flatter strangers, then all of you were in occupation, grand people with splendid equipages; I was powerless, I confess, tho more attached to my countrymen than you.

Two things, men of Athens, are characteristic of a well-disposed citizen—so may I speak of myself and give the least offense:—In authority, his constant aim should be the dignity and preeminence of the commonwealth; in all times and circumstances his spirit should be loyal. This depends upon nature; power and might upon other things. Such a spirit, you will find, I have ever sincerely cherished. Only see. When my person was demanded—when they brought Amphictyonic suits against me—when they menaced —when they promised—when they set these miscreants like wild beasts upon me—never in any way have I abandoned my affection for you. From the very beginning I chose an honest and straightforward course in politics, to support the honor, the power, the glory of my fatherland, these to exalt, in these to have been my being. I do not walk about the market-place gay and cheerful because the stranger has prospered, holding out my right hand and congratulating those who I think will report it yonder, and on any news of our own success shudder and groan and stoop to the earth, like these impious men, who rail at Athens, as if in so doing they did not rail at themselves; who look abroad, and if the foreigner thrives by the distresses of Greece, are thankful for it, and say we should keep him so thriving to all time.

Never, O ye gods, may those wishes be confirmed by you! If possible, inspire even in these men a better sense and feeling! But if they are indeed incurable, destroy them by themselves; exterminate them on land and sea; and for the rest of us, grant that we may speedily be released from our present fears, and enjoy a lasting deliverance![1]

---

[1] After the failure of Æschines in this prosecution, he went into exile and at Rhodes established a school of oratory. It is related of him that, one day when he had read this oration of Demosthenes to his students, it was received with such vociferous applause that Æschines generously remarked, "What would you not have said had you heard him thunder out the words himself?"

AESCHINES

AGAINST CTESIPHON; OR, ON THE CROWN [1]

(330 B.C.)

Born in 389 B.C., died in 314; served in several military campaigns; twice an envoy to Philip of Macedon; long the political antagonist of Demosthenes; after his defeat by Demosthenes, in the trial of Ctesiphon, went into exile.

You see, Athenians! what forces are prepared, what numbers formed and arrayed, what soliciting through the assembly, by a certain party; and all this to oppose the fair and ordinary course of justice in the state. As to me, I stand here in firm reliance, first on the immortal gods, next on the laws and you, convinced that faction never can have greater weight with you than law and justice.

It were to be wished, indeed, that the presidents of our senate and of our popular assembly would attend with due care to the order of their debates; that the laws ordained by Solon to secure the decency of public speaking might still preserve their force; that so our elder citizens might first arise in due and decent form (as these laws direct), without tumult or confusion, and each declare in order the salutary counsels

---

[1] Delivered in Athens 330 B.C. Translated by Thomas Leland. Abridged.

of his sage experience; that, after these, our other citizens who chose to speak might severally, and in order, according to their ages, propose their sentiments on every subject. Thus, in my opinion, would the course of government be more exactly regulated, and thus would our assemblies be less frequently engaged in trials.

But now, when these institutions, so confessedly excellent, have lost their force; when men propose illegal resolutions without reserve or scruple; when others are found to put them to the vote, not regularly chosen to preside in our assemblies, but men who have raised themselves to this dignity by intrigue; when if any of the other senators on whom the lot of presidency hath fairly fallen should discharge his office faithfully, and report your voices truly, there are men who threaten to impeach him, men who invade our rights, and regard the administration as their private property; who have secured their vassals, and raised themselves to sovereignty; who have suppressed such judicial procedures as are founded on established laws, and in the decision of those appointed by temporary decrees, consult their passions; now, I say, that most sage and virtuous proclamation is no longer heard, "Who is disposed to speak of those above fifty years old?" and then, "Who of the other citizens in their turns?" Nor is the indecent license of our speakers any longer restrained by our laws, by our magistrates; no, nor by the presiding tribe which contains a full tenth part of the community.

As to the general nature of this prosecution, thus far have I promised, and, I trust, without offense. Let me now request your attention to a few words about the laws relative to persons accountable to the public, which have been violated by the decree proposed by Ctesiphon.

In former times there were found magistrates of the most distinguished rank, and intrusted with the management of our revenues, who in their several stations were guilty of the basest corruption, but who, by forming an interest with the speakers in the senate and in the popular assembly, anticipated their accounts by public honors and declarations of applause. Thus, when their conduct came to a formal examination, their accusers were involved in great perplexity, their judges in still greater; for many of the persons thus subject to examination, tho convicted on the clearest evidence of having defrauded the public, were yet suffered to escape from justice; and no wonder. The judges were ashamed that the same man, in the same city, possibly in the same year, should be publicly honored in our festivals, that proclamation should be made "that the people had conferred a golden crown on him on account of his integrity and virtue"; that the same man, I say, in a short time after, when his conduct had been brought to an examination, should depart from the tribunal condemned of fraud. In their sentence, therefore, the judges were necessarily obliged to attend, not to the nature of those offenses, but to the reputation of the state.

Some of our magistrates, observing this, framed a law (and its excellence is undeniable) expressly forbidding any man to be honored with a crown whose conduct had not yet been submitted to the legal examination. But notwithstanding all the precaution of the framers of this law, pretenses were still found of force sufficient to defeat its intention. Of these you are to be informed, lest you should be unwarily betrayed into error. Some of those who, in defiance of the laws, have moved that men who yet stood accountable for their conduct should be crowned are still influenced by some degree of decency (if this can with propriety be said of men who purpose resolutions directly subversive of the laws); they still seek to cast a kind of veil on their shame. Hence are they sometimes careful to express their resolutions in this manner: "that the man whose conduct is not yet submitted to examination shall be honored with a crown when his accounts have first been examined and approved." But this is no less injurious to the state; for by these crowns and public honors is his conduct prejudiced and his examination anticipated, while the author of such resolutions demonstrates to his hearers that his proposal is a violation of the laws, and that he is ashamed of his offense. But Ctesiphon, my countrymen, hath at once broken through the laws relative to the examination of our magistrates; he hath scorned to recur to that subterfuge now explained; he hath moved you to confer a crown on Demosthenes previously to any examination of his conduct, at the very time while he was yet employed in the discharge of his magistracy.

But there is another evasion of a different kind to which they are to recur. These offices say they, to which a citizen is elected by an occasional decree, are by no means to be accounted magistracies, but commissions or agencies. Those alone are magistrates whom the proper officers appoint by lot in the temple of Theseus, or the people elect by suffrage in their ordinary assemblies, such as generals of the army, commanders of the cavalry, and such like; all others are but commissioners who are but to execute a particular decree. To this their plea I shall oppose your own law—a law enacted from a firm conviction that it must at once put an end to all such evasions. In this it is expressly declared that all offices whatever appointed by the voices of the people shall be accounted magistracies. In one general term the author of this law has included all. All has he declared "magistrates whom the votes of the assembly have appointed," and particularly "the inspectors of public works." Now Demosthenes inspected the repair of our walls, the most important of public works. "Those who have been intrusted with any public money for more than thirty days; those who are entitled to preside in a tribunal." But the inspectors of works are entitled to this privilege. What then does the law direct? That all such should assume not their "commission" but their "magistracy," having first been judicially approved (for even the magistrates appointed by lot are not exempted from this previous inquiry, but must be first approved before they assume their office). These are also directed by the law to submit the accounts of their administration to the legal officers, as well as every other magistrate. And for the truth of what I now advance, to the laws themselves do I appeal.

Here, then, you find that what these men call commissions or agencies are declared to be magistracies. It is your part to bear this in memory; to oppose the law to their presumption; to convince them that you are not to be influenced by the wretched sophistical artifice that would defeat the force of laws by words; and that the greater their address in defending their illegal proceedings, the more severely must they feel your resentment; for the public speaker should ever use the same language with the law. Should he at any time speak in one language, and the law pronounce another, to the just authority of law should you grant your voices, not to the shameless presumption of the speaker.

To that argument on which Demosthenes relies as utterly unanswerable I would now briefly speak. This man will say, "I am director of the fortifications. I confess it; but I have expended of my own money for the public service an additional sum of one hundred minæ, and enlarged the work beyond any instructions: for what then am I to account, unless a man is to be made accountable for his own beneficence? To this evasion you shall hear a just and good reply. In this city, of so ancient an establishment and a circuit so extensive, there is not a man exempted from account who has the smallest part in the affairs of state. This I shall show, first, in instances scarcely creditable: thus the priests and priestesses are by the laws obliged to account for the discharge of their office, all in general, and each in particular; altho they have received no more than an honorary pension, and have had no other duty but of offering up their prayers for us to the gods.

And this is not the case of single persons only, but of whole tribes as the Eumolpidæ, the Ceryces, and all the others. Again, the trierarchs are by the law made accountable for their conduct, altho no public money has been committed to their charge; altho they have not embezzled large portions of their revenue, and accounted but for a small part; altho they have not affected to confer bounties on you, while they really but restored your own property. No: they confessedly expended their paternal fortunes to approve their zealous affection for your service; and not our trierarchs alone, but the greatest assemblies in the state, are bound to submit to the sentence of our tribunals. First, the law directs that the council of the Areopagus shall stand accountable to the proper officers and submit their august transactions to a legal examination; thus our greatest judicial body stands in perpetual dependence on your decisions. Shall the members of this council, then, be precluded from the honor of a crown? Such has been the ordinance from times the most remote. And have they no regard to public honor? So scrupulous is their regard, that it is not deemed sufficient that their conduct should not be notoriously criminal; their least irregularity is severely punished—a discipline too rigorous for our delicate orators.

Again, our lawgiver directs that the senate of five hundred shall be bound to account for their conduct; and so great diffidence does he express of those who have not yet rendered such account, that in the very beginning of the law it is ordained "that no magistrate who has not yet passed through the ordinary examination shall be permitted to go abroad." But here a man may exclaim, "What! in the name of Heaven, am I, because I have been in office, to be confined to the city?" Yes, and with good reason; lest, when you have secreted the public money and betrayed your trust, you might enjoy your perfidy by flight. Again, the laws forbid the man who has not yet accounted to the state to dedicate any part of his effects to religious purposes, to deposit any offering in a temple, to accept of an adoption into any family, to make any alienation of his property; and to many other instances is the prohibition extended. In one word, our lawgiver has provided that the fortunes of such persons shall be secured as a pledge to the community until their accounts are fairly examined and approved. Nay, further: suppose there be a man who has neither received nor expended any part of the public money, but has only been concerned in some affairs relative to the state, even such a one is bound to submit his accounts to the proper officers. "But how can the man who has neither received nor expended pass such accounts?" The law has obviated this difficulty, and expressly prescribed the form of his accounts. It directs that it shall consist of this declaration: "I have not received, neither have I disposed of any public money." To confirm the truth of this hear the laws themselves.

When Demosthenes, therefore, shall exult in his evasion, and insist that he is not to be accountable for the additional sum which he bestowed freely on the state, press him with this reply: "It was then your duty, Demosthenes, to have permitted the usual and legal proclamation to be made, Who is disposed to prosecute? and to have given an opportunity to every citizen that pleased to have urged on his part that you bestowed no such additional sum; but that, on the contrary, having been intrusted with ten talents for the repair of our fortifications, you really expended but a small part of this great sum. Do not assume an honor to which you have no pretensions; do not wrest their suffrages from your judges; do not act in presumptuous contempt of the laws, but with due submission yield to their guidance. Such is the conduct that must secure the freedom of our constitution.''

As to the evasions on which these men rely, I trust that I have spoken sufficiently. That Demosthenes really stood accountable to the state at the time when this man proposed his decree, that he was really a magistrate, as manager of the theatrical funds; a magistrate, as inspector of the fortifications; that his conduct in either of these offices had not been examined, had not obtained the legal approbation, I shall now endeavor to demonstrate from the public records. Read in whose archonship, in what month, on what day, in what assembly, Demosthenes was chosen into the office of manager of the theatrical funds. So shall it appear, that during the execution of this office the decree was made which conferred this crown on him.

If, then, I should here rest my cause without proceeding further, Ctesiphon must stand convicted—convicted, not by the arguments of his accuser, but by the public records. In former times, Athenians, it was the custom that the state should elect a comptroller, who in every

presidency of each tribe was to return to the
people an exact state of the finances. But by
the implicit confidence which you reposed in
Eubulus, the men who were chosen to the management of the theatrical money executed this
office of comptroller (I mean before the law of
Hegemon was enacted), together with the offices
of receiver and of inspector of our naval affairs;
they were charged with the building of our
arsenals, with the repair of our roads; in a word,
they were intrusted with the conduct of almost
all our public business. I say not this to impeach their conduct or to arraign their integrity;
I mean but to convince you that our laws have expressly directed that no man yet accountable for
his conduct in any one office, even of the smallest
consequence, shall be entitled to the honor of
a crown until his accounts have been regularly
examined and approved; and that Ctesiphon has
yet presumed to confer this honor on Demosthenes when engaged in every kind of public magistracy. At the time of this decree he was a
magistrate as inspector of the fortifications, a
magistrate as intrusted with public money, and,
like other officers of the state, imposed fines and
presided in tribunals. These things I shall prove
by the testimony of Demosthenes and Ctesiphon
themselves; for in the archonship of Chærondas,
on the 22d of the month Thargelion, was a
popular assembly held, in which Demosthenes
obtained a decree appointing a convention of
the tribes on the 2d of the succeeding month;

and on the 3d his decree directed, still further, that supervisors should be chosen and treasurers from each tribe, for conducting the repairs of our fortifications. And justly did he thus direct, that the public might have the security of good and responsible citizens who might return a fair account of all disbursements. Read these decrees.

Yes; but you will hear it argued in answer, that to this office of inspector of the works he was not appointed in the general assembly either by lot or suffrage. This is an argument on which Demosthenes and Ctesiphon will dwell with the utmost confidence. My answer shall be easy, plain, and brief; but first I would premise a few things on this subject. Observe, Athenians! of magistracy there are three kinds: First, those appointed by lot or by election. Secondly, the men who have managed public money for more than thirty days, or have inspected public works. To these the law adds another species, and expressly declares that all such persons as, in consequence of a regular appointment, have enjoyed the right of jurisdiction, shall when approved be accounted magistrates: so that, should we take away the magistrates appointed by lot or suffrage, there yet remains the last kind of those appointed by the tribes, or the thirds of tribes, or by particular districts, to manage public money, all which are declared to be magistrates from the time of their appointment. And this happens in cases like that before us where it is a direction to the tribes to make canals or to build ships of war. For the truth of this I appeal to the laws themselves.

Let it be remembered that, as I have already observed, the sentence of the law is this, that all those appointed to any office by their tribes shall act as magistrates, when first judicially approved. But the Pandionian tribe has made Demosthenes a magistrate, by appointing him an inspector of the works; and for this purpose he has been intrusted with public money to the amount of near ten talents. Again, another law expressly forbids any magistrate who yet stands accountable for his conduct to be honored with a crown. You have sworn to give sentence according to the laws. Here is a speaker who has brought in a decree for granting a crown to a man yet accountable for his conduct. Nor has he added that saving clause, "when his accounts have first been passed." I have proved the point of illegality from the testimony of your laws, from the testimony of your decrees, and from that of the opposite parties. How then can any man support a prosecution of this nature with greater force and clearness?

But further, I shall now demonstrate that this decree is also a violation of the law by the manner in which it directs that this crown shall be proclaimed. The laws declare, in terms the most explicit, that if any man receives a crown from the senate, the proclamation shall be made in the senate-house; if by the people, in the assembly; never in any other place.

And this institution is just and excellent. The author of this law seems to have been persuaded that a public speaker should not ostentatiously display his merits before foreigners: that he should be contented with the approbation of this city, of these his fellow citizens, without practising vile arts to procure a public honor. So thought our lawgiver.

Since, then, it is provided that those crowned by the senate shall be proclaimed in the senate-house, those by the people in the assembly; since it is expressly forbidden that men crowned by their districts or by their tribes shall have proclamation made in the theater; that no man may indulge an idle vanity by public honors thus clandestinely procured; since the law directs, still further, that no proclamation shall be made by any others, but by the senate, by the people, by the tribes, or by the districts, respectively; if we deduct all these cases, what will remain but crowns conferred by foreigners? That I speak with truth the law itself affords a powerful argument. It directs that the golden crown conferred by proclamation in the theater shall be taken from the person thus honored and consecrated to Minerva. But who shall presume to impute so illiberal a procedure to the community of Athens? Can the state or can a private person be suspected of a spirit so sordid that when they themselves have granted a crown,

when it has been just proclaimed, they should
take it back again and dedicate it? No; I apprehend that such dedication is made because
the crown is conferred by foreigners, that no
man by valuing the affection of strangers at a
higher rate than that of his country, may suffer
corruption to steal into his heart. But when
a crown has been proclaimed in the assembly, is
the person honored bound to dedicate it? No;
he is allowed to possess it, that not he alone but
his posterity may retain such a memorial in their
family, and never suffer their affections to be
alienated from their country.

To enter into a minute examination of the
life of Demosthenes I fear might lead me into
a detail too tedious. And why should I insist
on such points as the circumstances of the indictment for his wound, brought before the Areopagus against Demomeles his kinsman, and the
gashes he inflicted on his own head? or why
should I speak of the expedition under Cephisodotus, and the sailing of our fleet to the Hellespont, when Demosthenes acted as a trierarch,
entertained the admiral on board his ship, made
him partaker of his table, of his sacrifices and
religious rites, confessed his just right to all
those instances of affection, as an hereditary
friend; and yet, when an impeachment had been
brought against him which affected his life,
appeared as his accuser? Why, again, should I
take notice of his affair with Midias; of the blows
which he received in his office of director of the

entertainments; or how, for the sum of thirty
minæ he compounded this insult, as well as the
sentence which the people pronounced against
Midias in the theater? These and the like particulars I determine to pass over; not that I
would betray the cause of justice; not that I
would recommend myself to favor by an affected
tenderness; but lest it should be objected that I
produce facts true, indeed, but long since acknowledged and notorious. Say then, Ctesiphon,
when the most heinous instances of this man's
baseness are so incontestably evident that his
accuser exposes himself to the censure, not of
advancing falsehoods, but of recurring to facts
so long acknowledged and notorious, is he to be
publicly honored, or to be branded with infamy?
And shall you, who have presumed to form decrees equally **contrary** to truth and to the laws,
insolently bid **defiance** to the tribunal, or feel
the weight of public justice?

My objections to his public conduct shall be
more explicit. I am informed that Demosthenes,
when admitted to his defense, means to enumerate four different periods in which he was
engaged in the administration of affairs. One,
and the first, of these (as I am assured) he
accounts that time in which we were at war with
Philip for Amphipolis; and this period he closes
with the peace and alliance which we concluded,
in consequence of the decree proposed by Philocrates, in which Demosthenes had equal share,
as I shall immediately demonstrate. The second

period he computes from the time in which we enjoyed this peace down to that day when he put an end to a treaty that had till then subsisted and himself proposed the decree for war. The third, from the time when hostilities were commenced, down to the fatal battle of Chæronea. The fourth is this present time.

After this particular specification, as I am informed, he means to call on me, and to demand explicitly on which of these four periods I found my prosecution, and at what particular time I object to his administration as inconsistent with the public interest. Should I refuse to answer, should I attempt the least evasion or retreat, he boasts that he will pursue me and tear off my disguise; that he will haul me to the tribunal, and compel me to reply. That I may then at once confound this presumption, and guard you against such artifice, I thus explicitly reply: Before these your judges, before the other citizens spectators of this trial, before all the Greeks who have been solicitous to hear the event of this cause (and of these I see no small number, but rather more than ever yet known to attend on any public trial) I thus reply: I say, that on every one of these four periods which you have thus distinguished is my accusation founded.

You had the fairest opportunity, Athenians! of concluding this first peace[1] in conjunction with

---

[1] Described by Æschines in an omitted paragraph as "That

the general assembly of the Greeks, had certain persons suffered you to wait the return of our ambassadors, at that time sent through Greece to invite the states to join in the general confederacy against Philip; and in the progress of these negotiations the Greeks would have freely acknowledged you the leading state. Of these advantages were you deprived by Demosthenes and Philocrates, and by the bribes which they received in traitorous conspiracy against your government. If at first view this assertion should seem incredible to any in this tribunal, let such attend to what is now to be advanced, just as men sit down to the accounts of money a long time since expended. We sometimes come from home possessed with false opinions of the state of such accounts; but when the several sums have been exactly collected, there is no man of a temper so obstinate as to dissemble or to refuse his assent to the truth of that which the account itself exhibits. Hear me in the present cause with dispositions of the same kind. And if with respect to past transactions any one among you has come hither possessed with an opinion that Demosthenes never yet appeared as advocate for the interests of Philip, in dark confederacy with Philocrates; if any man, I say, be so persuaded, let him suspend his judgment, and neither assent nor deny until he has heard (for justice requires this).

peace of which you Demosthenes and Philocrates were the first movers."

The prince whose gold purchased these important points is by no means to be accused. Before the treaty was concluded, and previously to his solemn engagements, we cannot impute it as a crime that he pursued his own interests; but the men who traitorously resigned into his hands the strength and security of the state should justly feel the severest effects of your resentment. He, then, who now declares himself the enemy of Alexander, Demosthenes, who at that time was the enemy of Philip—he who objects to me my connections of friendship with Alexander, proposed a decree utterly subversive of the regular and gradual course of public business, by which the magistrates were to convene an assembly on the eighth of the month Elaphebolion, a day destined to the sacrifices and religious ceremonies in honor of Esculapius, when the rites were just preparing.

After these festivals our assemblies were accordingly convened. In the first was the general resolution of our allies publicly read, the heads of which I shall here briefly recite. They in the first place, resolved that you should proceed to deliberate only about a peace. Of an alliance not one word was mentioned; and this not from inattention, but because they deemed even a peace itself rather necessary than honorable. In the next place, they wisely provided against the fatal consequences of the corruption of Demosthenes; for they expressly resolved still further, that "it shall and may be lawful for any of the Grecian states whatever, within the space of three months, to accede in due form to this treaty, to join in the same solemn engagements, and to be included in the same stipulations.'' Thus were two most important points secured: First, an interval of three months was provided for the Greeks—a time sufficient to prepare their deputations; and then the whole collected body of the nation stood well affected and attached to Athens, that if at any time the treaty should be violated, we might not be involved in war single and unsupported. These resolutions are themselves the amplest testimony to the truth of my assertions.

It remains that I produce some instances of his abandoned flattery. For one whole year did Demosthenes enjoy the honor of a senator; and yet in all that time it never appears that he moved to grant precedency to any ministers; for the first, the only time, he conferred this distinction on the ministers of Philip; he serviilely attended to accommodate them with his cushions and his carpets; by the dawn of day he conducted them to the theater; and by his indecent and abandoned adulation raised a universal uproar of derision. When they were on their departure toward Thebes he hired three teams of mules, and conducted them in state into that city. Thus did he expose his country to ridicule. But that I may confine myself to facts, read the decree relative to the grant of precedency.

And yet this abject, this enormous flatterer, when he had been the first that received advice of Philip's death, from the emissaries of Charidemus, pretended a divine mission, and, with a shameless lie, declared that this intelligence had been conveyed to him, not by Charidemus, but by Jupiter and Minerva! Thus he dared to boast that these divinities, by whom he had sworn falsely in the day, had condescended to hold communication with him in the night, and to inform him of futurity. Seven days had now scarcely elapsed since the death of his daughter, when this wretch, before he had performed the usual rites of mourning, before he had duly paid her funeral honors, crowned his head with a chaplet, put on his white robe, made a solemn sacrifice in despite of law and decency; and this when he had lost his child—the first, the only child that had ever called him by the tender name of father! I say not this to insult his misfortunes; I mean but to display his real character: for he who hates his children, he who is a bad parent cannot possibly prove a good minister. He who is insensible to that natural affection which should engage his heart to those who are most intimate and near to him can never feel a greater regard to your welfare than to that of strangers. He who acts wickedly in private life cannot prove excellent in his public conduct; he who is base at home can never acquit himself with honor when sent to a strange country in a public character; for it is not the man but the scene that changes.

When Philip, then, had possessed himself of Thermopylæ by surprise; when, contrary to all expectation, he had subverted the cities of the Phocians; when he had raised the state of Thebes to a degree of power too great (as we then thought) for the times or for our interest; when we were in such consternation that our effects were all collected from the country and deposited within these walls—the severest indignation was expressed against the deputies in general who had been employed in the negotiation of the peace, but principally, and above all others, against Philocrates and Demosthenes; because they had not only been concerned in the deputation, but were the first movers and authors of the decree for peace. It happened at this juncture that a difference arose between Demosthenes and Philocrates, nearly on the same occasion which you yourselves suspected must produce animosities between them. The ferment which arose from hence, together with the natural distemper of his mind, produced such counsels as nothing but an abject terror could dictate, together with a malignant jealousy of the advantages which Philocrates derived from his corruption. He concluded that by inveighing against his colleagues and against Philip, Philocrates must inevitably fall; that the other deputies must be in danger; that he himself must gain reputation; and notwithstanding his baseness and treachery to his friends, he must acquire the character of a consummate patriot. The enemies of our tranquillity perceived his designs: they at once invited him to the gallery, and extolled him as the only man who disdained to betray the public interest for a bribe. The moment he appeared he kindled up the flame of war and confusion. He it was, Athenians, who first found out the Serrian fort, and Doriscum, and Ergiske, and Murgiske, and Ganos, and Ganides—places whose very names were hitherto utterly unknown; and such was his power in perverting and perplexing, that if Philip declined to send his ministers to Athens, he represented it as a contemptuous insult on the state; if he did send them, they were spies and not ministers; if he inclined to submit his disputes with us to some impartial mediating state, no equal umpire could be found, he said, between us and Philip. This prince gave us up the Halonesus; but he insisted that we should not receive it unless it was declared, not that he *resigned*, but *restored*—thus caviling about syllables. And to crown all his conduct, by paying public honors to those who had carried their arms into Thessaly and Magnesia, under the command of Aristodemus, in direct violation of the treaty, he dissolved the peace, and prepared the way for calamity and war.

When he had finished he presented a decree to the secretary longer than the Iliad, more frivolous than the speeches which he usually de-

livers, or than the life which he has led; filled
with hopes never to be gratified, and with armaments never to be raised. And while he diverted
your attention from his fraud, while he kept
you in suspense by his flattering assurances, he
seized the favorable moment to make his grand
attack, and moved that ambassadors should be
sent to Eretria, who should entreat the Eretrians
(because such entreaties were mighty necessary)
not to send their contribution of five talents to
Athens, but to intrust it to Callias; again, he
ordained that ambassadors should be appointed
to repair to Oreum, and to prevail on that state
to unite with Athens in strict confederacy. And
now it appeared, that through this whole transaction he had been influenced by a traitorous
motive; for these ambassadors were directed to
solicit the people of Oreum also to pay their
five talents, not to you, but to Callias. To prove
the truth of this read the decree—not all the
pompous preamble, the magnificent account of
navies, the parade and ostentation; but confine
yourself to the point of fraud and circumvention, which were practised with too much success
by this impious and abandoned wretch, whom
the decree of Ctesiphon declares to have persevered, through the course of all his public
conduct, in an inviolable attachment to the
state.

Here is a grand account of ships and of
levies, of the full moon, and of conventions. Thus
were you amused by words; while in fact you

lost the contributions of your allies, you were defrauded of ten talents.

It remains that I inform you of the real motive which prompted Demosthenes to procure this decree; and that was a bribe of three talents —one received from Chalcis, by the hands of Callias, another from Eretia, by Clitarchus, the sovereign of this state; the third paid by Oreum, by which means the stipulation was discovered; for as Oreum is a free state, all things are there transacted by a public decree. And as the people of this city had been quite exhausted in the war with Philip, and reduced to the utmost indigence, they sent over Gnosidemus, who had once been their sovereign, to entreat Demosthenes to remit the talent, promising, on this condition, to honor him with a statue of bronze, to be erected in their city. He answered their deputy, that he had not the least occasion for their paltry brass; that he insisted on his stipulation, which Callias should prosecute. The people of Oreum, thus pressed by their creditor, and not prepared to satisfy him, mortgaged their public revenues to Demosthenes for this talent, and paid him interest at the rate of one drachma a month for each mina, until they were enabled to discharge the principal. And, to prove this, I produce the decree of the Oreitans.

Here is a decree, Athenians, scandalous to our country. It is no small indication of the general conduct of Demosthenes, and it is an evidence of the most flagrant kind, which must condemn Ctesiphon at once: for it is not possible that he who has descended to such sordid bribery can be that man of consummate virtue which Ctesiphon has presumed to represent him in his decree.

And what can be conceived surprising or extraordinary that we have not experienced? Our lives have not passed in the usual and natural course of human affairs: no, we were born to be an object of astonishment to posterity. Do we not see the King of Persia, he who opened a passage for his navy through Mount Athos, who stretched his bridge across the Hellespont, who demanded earth and water from the Greeks; he who in his letters presumed to style himself sovereign of mankind from the rising to the setting sun; now no longer contending to be lord over others, but to secure his personal safety? Do not we see those crowned with honor and ennobled with the command of the war against Persia who rescued the Delphian temple from sacrilegious hands? Has not Thebes, our neighboring state, been in one day torn from the midst of Greece? And, altho this calamity may justly be imputed to her own pernicious councils, yet we are not to ascribe such infatuation to any natural causes, but to the fatal influence of some evil genius. Are not the Lacedæmonians, those wretched men, who had but once slightly interfered in the sacrilegious outrage on the temple, who in their day of power aspired to the sovereignty of Greece, now reduced to display their wretchedness to the world by sending hostages to Alexander, ready to submit to that fate which he shall pronounce on themselves and on their country; to those terms which a conqueror, and an incensed conqueror, shall vouchsafe to grant? And is not this our state, the common refuge of the Greeks, once the great resort of all the ambassadors from the several cities, sent to implore our protection as their sure resource, now obliged to contend, not for sovereign authority, but for our native land? And to these circumstances have we been gradually reduced from that time when Demosthenes first assumed the administration.

And let it be observed that in these his negotiations he committed three capital offenses against the state. In the first place, when Philip made war on us only in name, but in reality pointed all his resentment against Thebes (as appears sufficiently from the event, and needs not any further evidence), he insidiously concealed this, of which it so highly concerned us to be informed; and pretending that the alliance now proposed was not the effect of the present conjuncture, but of his negotiations, he first prevailed on the people not to debate about conditions, but to be satisfied that the alliance was formed on any terms; and having secured this point, he gave up all Bœotia to the power of Thebes, by inserting this clause in the decree that if any city should revolt from the Thebans, the Athenians would grant their assistance to

such of the Bœotians only as should be resident
in Thebes; thus concealing his fraudulent designs
in spacious terms, and betraying us into his
real purposes, according to his usual practise;
as if the Bœotians, who had really labored under
the most grievous oppression, were to be fully
satisfied with the fine periods of Demosthenes,
and to forget all resentment of the wrongs which
they had suffered. Then as to the expenses of
the war, two thirds of these he imposed on us,
who were the farthest removed from danger,
and one third only on the Thebans; for which,
as well as all his other measures, he was amply
bribed. And with respect to the command, that
of the fleet he indeed divided between us; the
expense he imposed entirely on Athens; and that
of the land forces (if I am to speak seriously
I must insist on it) he absolutely transferred
to the Thebans; so that during this whole war
our general Stratocles had not so much authority
as might enable him to provide for the security
of his soldiers. And here I do not urge offenses
too trivial for regard of other men. No: I
speak them freely; all mankind condemn them,
and you yourselves are conscious of them, yet
will not be roused to resentment. For so completely has Demosthenes habituated you to his
offenses, that you now hear them without emo-
tion or surprise. But this should not be; they
should excite your utmost indignation, and
meet their just punishment, if you would preserve those remains of fortune which are still
left to Athens.

And here let us recall to mind those gallant men whom he forced out to manifest destruction, without one sacred rite happily performed, one propitious omen to assure them of success; and yet, when they had fallen in battle, presumed to ascend their monument with those coward feet that fled from their post, and pronounced his encomiums on their merit. But O thou who, on every occasion of great and important action, hast proved of all mankind the most worthless, in the insolence of language the most astonishing, canst thou attempt in the face of these thy fellow citizens to claim the honor of a crown for the misfortunes in which thou hast plunged thy city? Or, should he claim it, can you restrain your indignation, and has the memory of your slaughtered countrymen perished with them? Indulge me for a moment, and imagine that you are now not in this tribunal, but in the theater; imagine that you see the herald approaching, and the proclamation prescribed in this decree on the point of being delivered; and then consider whether will the friends of the deceased shed more tears at the tragedies, at the pathetic stories of the great characters to be presented on the stage, or at the insensibility of their country?

That I may now speak of the fourth period, and thus proceed to the present times, I must recall one particular to your thoughts: that Demosthenes not only deserted from his post in battle, but fled from his duty in the city, under the pretense of employing some of our ships in collecting contributions from the Greeks; but when, contrary to expectation, the public dangers seemed to vanish, he again returned. At first he appeared a timorous and dejected creature: he rose in the assembly, scarcely half alive, and desired to be appointed a commissioner for settling and establishing the treaty; but during the first progress of these transactions you did not even allow the name of Demosthenes to be subscribed to your decrees, but appointed Nausicles your principal agent; yet now he has the presumption to demand a crown. When Philip died and Alexander succeeded to the kingdom, then did he once more practise his impostures. He raised altars to Pausanias, and loaded the senate with the odium of offering sacrifices and public thanksgivings on this occasion. He called Alexander a margites, and had the presumption to assert that he would never stir from Macedon; for that he would be satisfied with parading through his capital, and there tearing up his victims in search of happy omens. "And this," said he, "I declare, not from conjecture, but from a clear conviction of this great truth, that glory is not to be purchased but by blood"; the wretch! whose veins have no blood; who judged of Alexander, not from the temper of Alexander, but from his own dastardly soul.

But when the Thessalians had taken up arms against us, and the young prince at first expressed the warmest resentment, and not without reason—when an army had actually infested

Thebes, then was he chosen our ambassador; but when he had proceeded as far as Cithæron he turned and ran back to Athens. Thus has he proved equally worthless, both in peace and in war. But what is most provoking, you refused to give him up to justice; nor would you suffer him to be tried in the general council of the Greeks; and if that be true which is reported, he has now repaid your indulgence by an act of direct treason; for the mariners of the Parhalian galley, and the ambassadors sent to Alexander, report (and with great appearance of truth) that there is one Aristion, a Platæan, the son of Aristobulus, the apothecary (if any of you know the man). This youth, who was distinguished by the beauty of his person, lived a long time in the house of Demosthenes; how he was there employed, or to what purposes he served, is a matter of doubt, and which it might not be decent to explain particularly; and, as I am informed, he afterward contrived (as his birth and course of life were a secret to the world) to insinuate himself into the favor of Alexander, with whom he lived with some intimacy. This man Demosthenes employed to deliver letters to Alexander, which served in some sort to dispel his fears, and effected his reconciliation with the prince, which he labored to confirm by the most abandoned flattery.

And now observe how exactly this account agrees with the facts which I allege against him; for if Demosthenes had been sincere in his pro-

fessions, had he really been that mortal foe to
Alexander, there were three most fortunate occasions for an opposition, not one of which he
appears to have improved. The first was when
this prince had but just ascended the throne,
and, before his own affairs were duly settled,
passed over into Asia, when the King of Persia
was in the height of all his power, amply furnished with ships, with money, and with forces,
and extremely desirous of admitting us to his
alliance, on account of the danger which then
threatened his dominions. Did you then utter
one word, Demosthenes? Did you rise up to
move for any one resolution? Am I to impute
your silence to terror—to the influence of your
natural timidity? But the interests of the state
cannot wait the timidity of a public speaker.
Again, when Darius had taken the field with
all his forces; when Alexander was shut up in
the defiles of Cilicia, and, as you pretended
destitute of all necessaries; when he was on the
point of being trampled down by the Persian
cavalry (this was your language); when your
insolence was insupportable to the whole city;
when you marched about in state with your
letters in your hands, pointing me out to your
creatures as a trembling and desponding wretch,
calling me the "gilded victim," and declaring
that I was to be crowned for sacrifice if any
accident should happen to Alexander: still were
you totally inactive; still you reserved yourself
for some fairer occasion.

I presume, then, it must be universally acknowledged that these are the characteristics of a friend to our free constitution: First, he must be of a liberal descent both by father and mother, lest the misfortune of his birth should inspire him with a prejudice against the laws which secure our freedom. Secondly, he must be descended from such ancestors as have done service to the people, at least from such as have not lived in enmity with them; this is indispensably necessary, lest he should be prompted to do the state some injury in order to revenge the quarrel of his ancestors. Thirdly, he must be discreet and temperate in his course of life, lest a luxurious dissipation of his fortune might tempt him to receive a bribe in order to betray his country. Fourthly, he must have integrity united with a powerful elocution; for it is the perfection of a statesman to possess that goodness of mind which may ever direct him to the most salutary measures, together with a skill and power of speaking which may effectually recommend them to his hearers; yet, of the two, integrity is to be preferred to eloquence. Fifthly, he must have a manly spirit, that in war and danger he may not desert his country. It may be sufficient to say, without further repetition, that a friend to the arbitrary power of a few is distinguished by the characteristics directly opposite to these.

And now consider which of them agree to Demosthenes. Let us state the account with the most scrupulous regard to justice. This man's father was Demosthenes of the Pæanian tribe, a citizen of repute (for I shall adhere strictly to truth). But how he stands as to family, with respect to his mother and her father, I must now explain. There was once in Athens a man called Gylon, who, by betraying Nymphæum in Pontus to the enemy, a city then possessed by us, was obliged to fly from his country in order to escape the sentence of death pronounced against him, and settled on the Bosphorus, where he obtained from the neighboring princes a tract of land called "The Gardens," and married a woman who indeed brought him a considerable fortune, but was by birth a Scythian; by her he had two daughters, whom he sent hither with a great quantity of wealth. One of them he settled—I shall not mention with whom, that I may not provoke the resentment of too many; the other Demosthenes the Pæanian married, in defiance of our laws, and from her is the present Demosthenes sprung—our turbulent and malicious informer. So that by his grandfather in the female line, he is an enemy to the state, for this grandfather was condemned to death by your ancestors; and by his mother he is a Scythian—one who assumes the language of Greece, but whose abandoned principles betray his barbarous descent.

And what has been his course of life? He first assumed the office of a triearch, and, having exhausted his paternal fortune by his ridiculous

vanity, he descended to the profession of a hired
advocate; but having lost all credit in this employment by betraying the secrets of his clients
to their antagonists, he forced his way into the
gallery, and appeared as a popular speaker.
When those vast sums of which he had defrauded the public were just dissipated, a sudden
tide of Persian gold poured into his exhausted
coffers; nor was all this sufficient for no fund
whatever can prove sufficient for the profligate and corrupt. In a word, he supported
himself, not by a fortune of his own, but by
your perils. But how does he appear with respect to integrity and force of elocution? Powerful in speaking, abandoned in his manners. Of
such unnatural depravity in his sensual grati-
fications that I can not describe his practises;
I cannot offend that delicacy to which such
shocking descriptions are always odious. And
how has he served the public? His speeches
have been plausible, his actions traitorous.

As to his courage, I need say but little on that
head. Did he himself deny that he is a coward?
Were you not sensible of it, I should think it
necessary to detain you by a formal course of
evidence; but as he has publicly confessed it
in our assemblies, and as you have been witnesses
of it, it remains only that I remind you of the
law enacted against such crimes. It was the
determination of Solon, our old legislator, that
he who evaded his duty in the field or left his
post in battle should be subject to the same

penalties with the man directly convicted of cowardice; for there are laws enacted against cowardice. It may, perhaps, seem wonderful that the law should take cognizance of a natural infirmity, but such is the fact. And why? That every one of us may dread the punishment denounced by the law more than the enemy, and thus prove the better soldier in the cause of his country. The man, then, who declines the service of the field, the coward, and he who leaves his post in battle, are by our lawgiver excluded from all share in public deliberations, rendered incapable of receiving the honor of a crown, and denied admission to the religious rites performed by the public. But you direct us to crown a person whom the laws declare to be incapable of receiving a crown; and by your decree you introduce a man into the theater who is disqualified from appearing there; you call him into a place sacred to Bacchus, who, by his cowardice, hath betrayed all our sacred places. But that I may not divert you from the great point, remember this: when Demosthenes tells you that he is a friend to liberty, examine not his speeches, but his actions; and consider not what he professes to be, but what he really is.

And now that I have mentioned crowns and public honors, while it yet rests on my mind, let me recommend this precaution. It will be your part, Athenians, to put an end to this frequency of public honors, these precipitate grants of crowns; else they who obtain them will owe you no acknowledgment, nor shall the state receive the least advantage; for you never can make bad men better, and those of real merit must be cast into the utmost dejection. Of this truth I shall convince you by the most powerful arguments. Suppose a man should ask at what time this state supported the most illustrious reputation—in the present days, or in those of our ancestors? With one voice you would reply, "In the days of our ancestors." At what time did our citizens display the greatest merit —then or now? They were then eminent; now, much less distinguished. At what time were rewards, crowns, proclamations, and public honors of every kind most frequent—then or now? Then they were rare and truly valuable; then the name of merit bore the highest luster; but now it is tarnished and effaced; while your honors are conferred by course and custom, not with judgment and distinction.

That you may conceive the force of what I here advance, I must explain myself still more clearly. Which, think ye, was the more worthy citizen—Themistocles, who commanded your fleet when you defeated the Persian in the seafight at Salamis, or this Demosthenes, who deserted from his post? Miltiades, who conquered the barbarians at Marathon, or this man? The chiefs who led back the people from Phyle? Aristides, surnamed the Just, a title quite different from that of Demosthenes? No; by the powers of Heaven. I deem the names of these heroes too noble to be mentioned in the same day with that of this savage. And let Demosthenes show, when he comes to his reply, if ever a decree was made for granting a golden crown to them. Was then the state ungrateful? No; but she thought highly of her own dignity. And these citizens, who were not thus honored, appear to have been truly worthy of such a state; for they imagined that they were not to be honored by public records, but by the memories of those they had obliged; and their honors have there remained from that time down to this day in characters indelible and immortal. There were citizens in those days, who, being stationed at the river Strymon, there patiently endured a long series of toils and dangers, and at length gained a victory over the Medes. At their return they petitioned the people for a reward; and a reward was conferred on them (then deemed of great importance) by erecting three Mercuries of stone in the usual portico, on which, however, their names were not inscribed, lest this might seem a monument erected to the honor of the commanders, not to that of the people.

As to the calumnies with which I am attacked, I would prevent their effect by a few observations. I am informed that Demosthenes is to urge that the state hath received services from him, but in many instances hath been injured by me; the transactions of Philip, the conduct of Alexander, all the crimes by them committed, he means to impute to me. And so much doth

he rely on his powerful abilities in the art of
speaking that he does not confine his accusations
to any point of administration in which I may
have been concerned; to any counsels which I
may have publicly suggested; he traduces the
retired part of my life, he imputes my silence
as a crime. And that no one topic may escape
his officious malice, he extends his accusations
even to my conduct when associated with my
young companions in our schools of exercise.
The very introduction of his defense is to con-
tain a heavy censure of this suit. I have commenced the prosecution, he will say, not to serve
the state, but to display my zeal to Alexander,
and to gratify the resentment of this prince
against him. And (if I am truly informed) he
means to ask why I now condemn the whole of
his administration, altho I never opposed, never
impeached any one part of it separately; and
why after a long course of time, in which I
scarcely ever was engaged in public business, I
now return to conduct this prosecution?

I, on my part, am by no means inclined to
emulate that course of conduct which Demosthenes hath pursued; nor am I ashamed of mine
own. Whatever speeches I have made, I do not
wish them unsaid; nor, had I spoken like Demosthenes, could I support my being. My silence, Demosthenes, hath been occasioned by
my life of temperance. I am contented with a
title; nor do I desire any accession which must
be purchased by iniquity. My silence, there-

fore, and my speaking are the result of reason, not extorted by the demands of inordinate passions. But you are silent when you have received your bribe; when you have spent it you exclaim. And you speak not at such times as you think fittest—not your own sentiments—but whenever you are ordered, and whatever is dictated by those masters whose pay you receive. So that without the least sense of shame you boldly assert what in a moment after is proved to be absolutely false. This impeachment, for instance, which is intended not to serve the state, but to display my officious zeal to Alexander, was actually commenced while Philip was yet alive, before ever Alexander had ascended the throne, before you had seen the vision about Pausanias, and before you had held your nocturnal interviews with Minerva and Juno. How then could I have displayed my zeal to Alexander, unless we had all seen the same visions with Demosthenes?

But, O ye gods! how can I restrain my indignation at one thing which Demosthenes means to urge (as I have been told), and which I shall here explain? He compares me to the Sirens, whose purpose is not to delight their hearers, but to destroy them. Even so, if we are to believe him, my abilities in speaking, whether acquired by exercise or given by nature, all tend to the detriment of those who grant me their attention. I am bold to say that no man hath a right to urge an allegation of this nature against me;

for it is shameful in an accuser not to be able
to establish his assertions with full proof. But
if such must be urged, surely it should not come
from Demosthenes; it should be the observation
of some military man, who had done important
services, but was unskilled in speech; who re-
pined at the abilities of his antagonist, conscious
that he could not display his own actions, and
sensible that his accuser had the art of persuading his audience to impute such actions to
him as he never had committed. But when a
man composed entirely of words, and these the
bitterest and most pompously labored—when he
recurs to simplicity, to artless facts, who can
endure it? He who is but an instrument, take
away his tongue, and he is nothing.

I am utterly at a loss to conceive, and would
gladly be informed, Athenians, on what grounds
you can possibly give sentence for the defendant.
Can it be because this decree is not illegal? No
public act was ever more repugnant to the laws.
Or because the author of this decree is not a
proper object of public justice? All your exam-
inations of men's conduct are no more, if this
man be suffered to escape. And is not this lamentable, that formerly your stage was filled
with crowns of gold, conferred by the Greeks on
the people (as the season of our public entertainments was assigned for the honors granted by
foreigners); but now, by the ministerial conduct
of Demosthenes, you should lose all crowns, all
public honors, while he enjoys them in full

pomp? Should any of these tragic poets whose works are to succeed our public proclamations represent Thersites crowned by the Greeks, no man could endure it, because Homer marks him as a coward and a sycophant; and can you imagine that you yourselves will not by the decision of all Greece of this man be permitted to receive his crown? In former times your fathers ascribed everything glorious and illustrious in the public fortune to the people; transferred the blame of everything mean and dishonorable to bad ministers. But now Ctesiphon would persuade you to divest Demosthenes of his ignominy, and to cast it on the state. You acknowledge that you are favored by fortune; and justly, for you are so favored; and will you now declare by your sentence that fortune hath abandoned you; that Demosthenes hath been your only benefactor? Will you proceed to the last absurdity, and in the very same tribunals condemn those to infamy whom you have detected in corruption; and yet confer a crown on him whose whole administration you are sensible hath been one series of corruption? In our public spectacles, the judges of our common dancers are at once fined if they decide unjustly; and will you who are appointed judges, not of dancing, but of the laws, and of public virtue, confer honors not agreeably to the laws, not on a few, and those most eminent in merit, but on any man who can establish his influence by intrigue?

And here, in your presence, would I gladly

enter into a discussion with the author of this decree, as to the nature of those services for which he desires that Demosthenes should be crowned. If you allege, agreeably to the first clause of the decree, that he hath surrounded our walls with an excellent intrenchment, I must declare my surprise. Surely the guilt of having rendered such a work necessary far outweighs the merits of its execution. It is not he who hath strengthened our fortifications, who hath digged our intrenchments, who hath disturbed the tombs of our ancestors, that should demand the honors of a patriotic minister, but he who hath procured some intrinsic services to the state. If you have recourse to the second clause, where you presume to say that he is a good man, and hath ever persevered in speaking and acting for the interest of the people, strip your decree of its vainglorious pomp; adhere to facts; and prove what you have asserted. I shall not press you with the instances of his corruption in the affairs of Amphissa and Eubœa. But if you attempt to transfer the merit of the Theban alliance to Demosthenes, you but impose on the men who are strangers to affairs, and insult those who are acquainted with them, and see through your falsehood. By suppressing all mention of the urgent juncture, of the illustrious reputation of these our fellow citizens, the real causes of this alliance, you fancy that you have effectually concealed your fraud in ascribing a merit to Demosthenes which really belongs to the state.

But to urge the point of greatest moment: should any of your sons demand by what examples they are to form their lives, how would you reply? For you well know that it is not only by bodily exercises, by seminaries of learning, or by instructions in music, that our youth are trained, but much more effectually by public examples. Is it proclaimed in the theater that a man is honored with a crown for his virtue, his magnanimity, and his patriotism, who yet proves to be abandoned and profligate in his life? The youth who sees this is corrupted. Is public justice inflicted on a man of base and scandalous vices like Ctesiphon? This affords excellent instruction to others. Doth the judge who has given a sentence repugnant to honor and to justice return home and instruct his son? That son is well warranted to reject his instruction. Advice in such a case may well be called impertinence. Not then as judges only, but as guardians of the state, give your voices in such a manner that you may approve your conduct to those absent citizens who may inquire what hath been the decision. You are not to be informed, Athenians, that the reputation of our country must be such as theirs who receive its honors. And surely it must be scandalous to stand in the same point of view, not with our ancestors, but with the unmanly baseness of Demosthenes.

Think on this critical season, in which you are to give your voices. In a few days the Pythian games are to be celebrated, and the convention of Grecian states to be collected. There shall our state be severely censured on account of the late measures of Demosthenes. Should you crown him, you must be deemed accessories to those who violated the general peace: if, on the contrary, you reject the demand, you will clear the state from all imputation. Weigh this clause maturely, as the interest, not of a foreign state, but of your own, and do not lavish your honors inconsiderately: confer them with a scrupulous delicacy; and let them be the distinctions of exalted worth and merit: nor be contented to hear, but look around you, where your own interest is so intimately concerned, and see who are the men that support Demosthenes. Are they his former companions in the chase, his associates in the manly exercises of his youth? No, by the Olympian god! he never was employed in rousing the wild boar, or in any such exercises as render the body vigorous; he was solely engaged in the sordid arts of fraud and circumvention.

And let not his arrogance escape your attention, when he tells you that by his embassy he wrested Byzantium from the hands of Philip; that his eloquence prevailed on the Acarnanians to revolt; his eloquence transported the souls of the Thebans. He thinks that you are sunk to such a degree of weakness that he may prevail on you to believe that you harbor the very genius of persuasion in your city, and not a vile sycophant. And when at the conclusion of his

defense he calls up his accomplices in corruption
as his advocates, then imagine that you see the
great benefactors of your country in this place
from whence I speak, arrayed against the villainy
of those men: Solon, the man who adorned our
free constitution with the noblest laws, the phil-
osopher, the renowned legislator, entreating you,
with that decent gravity which distinguished his
character, by no means to pay a greater regard
to the speeches of Demosthenes than to your
oaths and laws: Aristides, who was suffered to
prescribe to the Greeks their several subsidies,
whose daughters received their portions from
the people at his decease, roused to indignation
at this insult on public justice, and asking
whether you are not ashamed, that when your
fathers banished Arthmius the Zelian, who
brought in gold from Persia; when they were
scarcely restrained from killing a man connected
with the people in the most sacred ties, and by
public proclamation forbade him to appear in
Athens, or in any part of the Athenian territory;
yet you are going to crown Demosthenes with a
golden crown, who did not bring in gold from
Persia, but received bribes himself, and still possesses them. And can you imagine but that
Themistocles, and those who fell at Marathon,
and those who died at Platæa, and the very sepulchers of our ancestors, must groan if you confer a crown on this man, who confessedly united
with the Barbarians against the Greeks?

And now bear witness for me, thou earth, thou

sun, O virtue, and intelligence, and thou, O erudition, that teacheth us the just distinction between vice and goodness, I have stood up, I have spoken in the cause of justice. If I have supported my prosecution with a dignity befitting its importance, I have spoken as my wishes dictated; if too deficiently, as my abilities admitted. Let what hath now been offered, and what your own thoughts must supply, be duly weighed, and pronounce such a sentence as justice and the interests of the state demand.

DINARCHUS

AGAINST DEMOSTHENES [1]

(324 B.C.)

Born in Corinth in 361 B.C., died in 291; conspicuous as an orator
after the great masters had passed away; three only of his orations
have survived.

THUS your minister, Athenians! who hath pronounced sentence of death on himself should he
be convicted of receiving anything from Harpalus—this very man hath been clearly convicted
of accepting bribes from those whom in former
times he affected to oppose with so much zeal.
As Stratocles hath spoken largely on this subject; as many articles of accusation have been
anticipated; as the council of Areopagus hath
made a report on this inquiry so consonant to
equity and truth—a report confirmed and enforced by Stratocles, who hath produced the de-

[1] Abridged. Thomas Leland, the translator of this oration, introduces it with the following interesting note: "The occasion is dis-
tinctly recounted by Plutarch, who informs us that, some time after
the famous contest about the crown, in which Demosthenes gained
so complete a triumph over his rival Æschines, one Harpalus, who
had been in the service of Alexander, fled to Athens with the remains of an immense fortune, which had been dissipated by his
luxury, and there sought refuge from the anger of his master,
whose severity toward his favorites alarmed and prompted him to
this flight. The orators received his money, and labored to gain
him the protection of the state. Demosthenes, on the contrary,
urged to his countrymen the danger of exposing themselves to an
unnecessary and unjustifiable war by entertaining this fugitive.

crees enacted against these crimes—it remains that we who are now to speak (who are engaged in a cause of more importance than ever came before this state) should request the whole assembly, first, that we obtain your pardon if we should repeat some things already urged (for here our purpose is, not to abuse your patience, but to inflame your indignation); and, secondly, that you may not give up the general rights and laws of the community, or exchange the general welfare for the speeches of the accused. You see that in this assembly it is Demosthenes that is tried; in all other places your own trial is depending. On you men turn their eyes, and wait with eagerness to see how far the interests of your country will engage your care; whether you are to take on yourselves the corruption and iniquity of these men, or whether you are to manifest to the world a just resentment against those who are bribed to betray the state.

And altho the dignity and propriety of this

Harpalus, however, found means to soften his severity by a present of a magnificent vase, accompanied with twenty talents; and when it was expected that Demosthenes would have exerted his abilities in the Assembly against Harpalus, he pleaded indisposition, and was silent. This is the sum of Plutarch's account. But Pausanias, who seems to have conceived a more favorable opinion of the integrity of Demosthenes, observed, as a proof of his innocence, that an authentic account was sent to Athens, after the death of Harpalus, of all the sums distributed by him in this city and of the persons to whom each was paid; and that in this account no mention was at all made of Demosthenes, altho Philoxenus, who procured it, was his particular enemy, as well as Alexander. But, however this may be, the rumor of Harpalus's practises, and the report of the corrup-

procedure have received the approbation of the people, Demosthenes has recourse to complaints, to appeals, to malicious accusations, now that he finds himself convicted of receiving twenty talents of gold. Shall then this council, on whose faith and justice we rely, even in the important case of premeditated murder, to whom we commit the vengeance due to this crime, who have an absolute power over the persons and lives of our citizens, who can punish every violation of our laws, either by exile or by death— shall this council, I say, on an inquiry into a case of bribery, at once lose all its authority? "Yes; for the Areopagus hath reported falsely of Demosthenes." Extravagant and absurd! What! report falsely of Demosthenes and Demades, against whom even the truth seems scarcely to be declared with safety? You who have in former times moved that this council should take cognizance of public affairs, and have applauded their reports; you, whom this whole city hath not been able to restrain within the bounds of justice, hath the council reported falsely against you? Why then did you declare to the people that you were ready to submit to death if condemned by the report of this council? Why

tion of Demosthenes in particular, raised a considerable ferment at Athens."

To this statement by Mr. Leland may be added a paragraph from the sketch of Dinarchus that appears in the "Encyclopedia Britannica": "It must always be borne in mind that Dinarchus was a Corinthian, a mere resident alien at Athens, whose sympathies were in favor of Athenian oligarchy under Macedonian control. Little

have you availed yourself of their authority to take off so many of our citizens? Or whither shall we have recourse? to whom shall we intrust the detection of secret villainy? if you, notwithstanding all your affected regard to our popular government, are to dissolve this council, to whose protection our lives have been intrusted; to whose protection our liberty and our constitution have oftentimes been intrusted; by whose protection that person of thine hath been preserved (for, as you pretend, it hath frequently been attempted) to utter these calumnies against them; to whose care we have committed our secret archives, on which the very being of our state depends.

Has then Greece but slight, but common injuries to urge against Demosthenes and his sordid avarice? Hath the man so highly criminal the least pretense to mercy? Do not his late and former offenses call for the severest punishment? The world will hear the sentence you are this day to pronounce. The eyes of all men are fixed on you, impatient to learn the fate of so notorious a delinquent. You are they who, for crimes infinitely less heinous than his, have heavily and inexorably inflicted punishments on many. Menon was by you condemned to death for having

in the man's life, so far as we know it, enjoys our respect or esteem; his position must, at least, be broadly distinguished from that of such a man as Æschines, an Athenian citizen, who, while his city could still be served, abetted its enemies; or, from that of such a hireling as Demades. In the Harpalus affair Demosthenes was, beyond all reasonable doubt, innocent, and so probably were others of the accused."

subjected a free youth of Pallæne to his servile offices. Themistius, the Amphidnæan, who had abused a Rhodian woman that performed on the harp in the Eleusinian ceremonies, was by you condemned to death. The same sentence you pronounced on Euthymachus for prostituting a maiden of Olynthus. And now hath this traitor furnished all the tents of the Barbarians with the children and wives of the Thebans. A city of our neighbors and our allies hath been torn from the very heart of Greece. The plower and the sower now traverse the city of the Thebans, who united with us in the war against Philip. I say, the plower and the sower traverse their habitations; nor hath this hardened wretch discovered the least remorse at the calamities of a people to whom he was sent as our ambassador; with whom he lived, conversed, and enjoyed all that hospitality could confer; whom he pretends to have himself gained to our alliance; whom he frequently visited in their prosperity, but basely betrayed in their distress.

From the moment that he first began to direct our affairs, hath any one instance of good fortune attended us? Hath not all Greece, and not this state alone, been plunged in dangers, calamities, and disgrace? Many were the fair occasions which occurred to favor his administration; and all these occasions, of such moment to our interests, did he neglect. When any friend to his country, any useful citizen, attempted to do us service, so far was this leader, who is impatient to boast of his great actions, from cooperating with such men, that he instantly infected them with the contagion of his unhappy conduct.

Is it not scandalous, Athenians! that your opinion of the guilt of Demosthenes should depend only on our representations? Do you not know that he is a corrupted traitor, a public robber, false to his friends, and a disgrace to the state? What decrees, what laws have not been made subservient to his gain? There are men in this tribunal who were of the Three Hundred when he proposed the law relative to our trierarchs. Inform those who stand near you how, for a bribe of three talents, he altered and new-modeled this law in every assembly; and, just as he was feed, inserted or erased clauses. Say, in the name of Heaven! think ye, O men of Athens! that he gained nothing by his decree which gave Diphilus the honors of public maintenance and a statue? Was he not paid for obtaining the freedom of our city to Chærephilus, and Phidon, and Pamphilus, and Philip, and such mean persons as Epigenes and Conon? Was it for nothing he procured brazen statues to Berisades and Satyrus, and Gorgippus, those detested tyrants, from whom he annually receives a thousand bushels of corn, altho he is ready to lament the distresses of his fortune? Was it for nothing he made Taurosthenes an Athenian citizen, who enslaved his countrymen, and, together with his brother Callias, betrayed all Eubœa to Philip? whom our laws forbid to appear in Athens on pain of suffering the punishment of those who return from exile. Such a man this friend to our constitution enrolled among our citizens. These and many other instances in which he hath prostituted our honors can be proved by authentic evidence. And could he who gladly descended to small gains resist the temptation of so great a sum as twenty talents?

To what cause, Athenians! is the prosperity or the calamity of a state to be ascribed? To none so eminently as to its ministers and generals. Turn your eyes to the state of Thebes. It subsisted once; it was once great; it had its soldiers and commanders. There was a time (our elder citizens declare it, and on their authority I speak) when Pelopidas led the Sacred Band; when Epaminondas and his colleages commanded the army. Then did the Thebans gain the victory at Leuctra; then did they pierce into the territories of Lacedæmon, before deemed inaccessible; then did they achieve many and noble deeds. The Messenians they reinstated in their city, after a dispersion of four hundred years. To the Arcadians they gave freedom and independence; while the world viewed their illustrious conduct with applause. On the other hand, at what time did they act ignobly, unworthy of their native magnanimity? When Timolaus called himself Philip's friend, and was corrupted by his gold; when the traitor Phoxenus led the mercenary forces collected for the expedition to Amphissa; when Theagenes, wretched and corrupt, like this man, was made commander of their band; then did these three men confound and utterly destroy the affairs of that state and of all Greece. So indisputably true it is that leaders are the great cause of all the good and all the evil that can attend a community. We see this in the instance of our own state. Reflect, and say at what time was this city great and eminent in Greece, worthy of our ancestors, and of their illustrious action? when Conon (as our ancient citizens inform us) gained the naval victory at Cnidos; when Iphicrates cut off the detachment of the Lacedæmonians, when Chabrias defeated the Spartan fleet at Naxos; when Timotheus triumphed in the sea-fight near Corcyra. Then, Athenians! then it was that the Lacedæmonians, whose wise and faithful leaders, whose adherence to their ancient institutions had rendered them illustrious, were reduced so low as to appear before us, like abject supplicants, and implore for mercy. Our state, which they had subverted, by means of those who then conducted our affairs, once more became the sovereign of Greece; and no wonder, when the men now mentioned were our generals, and Archinus and Cephalus our ministers. For what is the great security of every state and nation? Good generals and able ministers.

Let this be duly and attentively considered, and let us no longer suffer by the corrupt and wretched conduct of Demosthenes. Let it not be imagined that we shall ever want good men and faithful counselors. With all the generous severity of our ancestors, let us exterminate the man whose bribery, whose treason, are evidently detected; who could not resist the temptation of gold; who hath involved his country in calamities the most grievous; let us destroy this pest of Greece; let not his contagion infect our city; then may we hope for some change of fortune, then may we expect that our affairs will flourish.

And now, my fellow citizens, consider how you are to act. The people have returned to you an information of a crime lately committed. Demosthenes stands first before you to suffer the punishment denounced against all whom this information condemns. We have explained his guilt with an unbiased attention to the laws; will you then discover a total disregard of all these offenses? Will you, when intrusted with so important a decision, invalidate the judgment of the people, of the Areopagus, of all mankind? Will you take on yourselves the guilt of these men? or will you give the world an example of that detestation in which this state holds traitors and hirelings that oppose our interests for a bribe? This entirely depends on you.

Despising, then, the entreaties, the false artifices of this man, let justice and integrity be your only objects. Consider the good of your country, not that of Demosthenes. This is the part of honest, upright judges. And should any man rise to plead in favor of Demosthenes, consider that such a man, if not involved in the same guilt, is at least disaffected to the state; as he would screen those from justice who have been bribed to betray its interests; as he would subvert the authority of the Areopagus, on which our lives depend, and confound and destroy all our laws and institutions.